Wiltshire

M-723 $19.95

MAKING THE SCENE

SETTING THE STAGE FOR SUCCESS

BY MICHAEL GALLINA

INFORMATION

Library of Congress Catalog Card Number: 92-61609

ISBN # 0-8256-6050-5

To my parents, Antoinette and Michael Gallina.

This dedication is but a small gesture to acknowledge my gratitude for the many years that my parents freely gave of themselves while asking nothing in return.

TABLE OF CONTENTS

TABLE OF CONTENTS

LIST OF ILLUSTRATIONS

LIST OF ILLUSTRATIONS

ACKNOWLEDGEMENTS

Had it not been for the support and encouragement provided by my wife **Jill Gallina**, this book would not have become a reality. From its early inception, Jill recognized the need for a book specifically written to assist directors of children's theater. Her continued reassurance of this need motivated me to begin the lengthy, yet rewarding, process required to gather and integrate the information contained within. Along with her moral support, Jill made every effort to free me from a number of daily tasks and obligations that would have impeded my ability to complete this project. While embracing a firm belief in the success of this concept, Jill provided me with the day-to-day assistance and encouragement needed to achieve my objective.

As a result of the faith **Tom Janssen** placed in me and this endeavor, I was able to proceed with confidence. As both a friend and the Creative Director of Educational Choral Music for Shawnee Press, Tom not only painstakingly edited each submission, he carefully orchestrated the efforts of Shawnee's excellent support staff. His experience as a choral director and educator proved to be an invaluable asset to the content and focus of this book. His vigilance, patience, and sincerity contributed greatly to the outcome of this project.

Assembling illustrations and multiple sections of text into an artistically and technically meaningful whole is a challenging and time-consuming undertaking. Thanks to the efforts of **Cathy Ciccarelli**, this process was completed in a creative and timely manner. In her capacity as Director of Art and Design, Cathy not only compiled the various sections of this book, she also gave freely of her talents to compose a creative and practical format. This significant contribution has proven to be a very valuable asset.

Mark DeHaven is an outstanding artist whose talents extend well beyond the confines of this project. His creative renditions of props and scenery clearly demonstrate the skills he possesses. In the process of transforming my technical drawings and plans into concise, well-defined illustrations, Mark exhibited both patience and a sincere desire to accurately represent the concepts I wished to convey. His special talents have greatly enhanced the information presented within.

Krista Hoell, literally "has a way with words." Her meticulous review of the text made it possible for us to provide you with a book that is easily readable. Krista's work on this project added many hours to her already demanding role as Shawnee Press Director of Advertising and Promotions. I am thankful for Krista's willingness to share her valuable and specialized skills with the other members of our editorial team.

Not only did the professional team at Shawnee Press provide artistic and technical assistance, they willingly modified personal schedules and production time frames in order to accommodate my needs. Their unselfish commitment to this endeavor is both recognized and appreciated.

Gratefully I acknowledge the contributions these people have made and extend my appreciation to them for their support and encouragement.

M. G.

"I don't have enough time or money to make involved sets and props! If I'm going to get a production on stage, I've got to stick to the basics."

As an educator and composer of children's musicals, I have frequently met teachers and directors who have shared these sentiments with me. They represent a number of dedicated individuals whose exceptional efforts have made it possible for young people to experience the joy and the magic of theater. Despite tight budgets and limited time, these determined directors continue to do commendable jobs. Many are convinced their productions will not become realities if too much energy is devoted to the creation of scenery and props.

The main purpose of this book is to demonstrate how easily directors can create quality staging, scenery, and props without diverting time and resources away from other aspects of their productions. Our schools, church and synagogue halls, camps, and recreational facilities are veritable storehouses of objects that can be appropriated easily for use within productions. In the rush to get a production on stage, these readily available items are frequently ignored or overlooked. For example, a rolling metal chair rack used to store folding chairs can also be used as a basic frame to support a rolling prop. With the simple addition of a sleigh-shaped cardboard cut-out, the rolling chair rack can depict a gliding entrance by Santa and his sleigh. This useful piece of seemingly unrelated equipment can be modified to create numerous stage illusions. In the chapter devoted to

"Common Items/Uncommon Uses," you will find directions explaining how this item, as well as many other pieces of common equipment, can be transformed into useful theatrical props.

Along with the need to find inexpensive methods for making props and scenery, overworked directors frequently bemoan the fact that limitations on their time make it next to impossible for them to competently address set construction. In the chapter entitled "Getting the Job Done," this book identifies a number of tried-and-true approaches which have made it possible for directors to focus on other production needs while using the skills of volunteers to handle scenery. In addition to suggestions on how to get the job done, the chapter on "Specialty Sets" presents a number of options for sets that can be easily constructed and stored for future productions. These sets are generic in design and can be adapted readily to a wide range of productions.

Staging options presented by each performance hall are significant factors which contribute to the quality of a production. Based upon conversations with directors I have met, it appears that 9 out of every 10 conduct productions in areas not resembling a formal stage. It is quite understandable why these unique conditions present countless staging challenges. Facilities in schools and houses of worship which have been designated as "All-Purpose Rooms" are frequently so dysfunctional, they might as well be referred to as "No-Purpose Rooms!" It is regrettable that many of the productions presented by children

INTRODUCTION

are performed in all-purpose rooms and gymnasiums, but there is definitely a bright side to this situation. Many of the areas not intentionally designed for stage performances, provide some very unique opportunities for special effects, dramatic entrances, audience involvement, and much more. Chapter I entitled "Taking Advantage of Your Performance Hall" presents a range of options available when productions must be staged in facilities not originally designed for performances.

This book has been designed to provide quick and simple suggestions for creating engaging scenery and props while still accommodating the busy schedules of most teachers and directors. Descriptive chapter headings and clearly drawn illustrations provide easy access to the required information. It is not necessary to read the chapters in the sequence in which they appear. Readers are encouraged to go directly to the chapters addressing their most immediate needs.

> (?) **In order to construct the scenery and props contained within, it will be necessary to use basic hand tools along with some power tools. With this in mind, a safety symbol has been incorporated into the text and illustrations. When the outline of a stop sign containing a question mark appears, special thought should be given to safety. The question mark represents the following questions: 1.) "Have I taken all safety precautions?" 2.) "Can I proceed safely?"**

There are many scholarly and technical publications devoted to the creation of scenery intended for use in the professional theater. The materials and designs discussed within those books are usually representative of what, in actuality, is a very specialized field. Often, the typical director of children's theater has neither the time, money, nor appropriate facilities to take advantage of what is suggested in those professional texts.

This book is intended to serve the needs of the teacher or director who works in a school or similar setting. The suggestions are intended for amateur theater productions. The required materials and tools can be found readily in local hardware stores and lumberyards. Instead of supplies found exclusively in theatrical supply houses, materials noted within this book can usually be obtained from school stockrooms and local retail stores.

Given the limited resources accessible to directors of amateur and children's theater, this book is intended to provide options congruent with available resources. Fully realizing the substantial amount of time, energy, and talent dedicated professionals devote to student theatrical productions, I hope this book will lend valuable support to their laudable efforts.

Mike Gallina

Many of the costumes and sets that Jill and Michael have incorporated into Gallina musicals have been designed in their backyard workshop.

In collaboration with his wife Jill, Michael Gallina has written over 20 musical plays for children. These plays address a broad spectrum of topics ranging from the more serious subject of substance abuse, to light-hearted musicals involving humorous thematic material. Wide World Music, Jenson Publications, Hal Leonard Publications, Kimbo Educational, Educational Activities, Smithsonian Publications, and most recently, Shawnee Press have been among the publishers which have produced and recorded the music written by the Gallinas.

Along with their active involvement in the creation of musicals for children, Jill and Michael have traveled extensively in the United States and Canada. The purpose of their travel has been to conduct musical workshops for educators and leaders of youth organizations. In conjunction with the numerous workshops they have presented, the Gallinas have come in contact with literally thousands of music teachers and directors. As a result of their contact and interaction with educators who bring musicals and plays to children, Jill and Michael have become conversant with the talents and needs of these dedicated individuals.

Along with their educational travels, the Gallinas have had many opportunities to see their musical productions performed all across the country. They also receive video tapes of productions that have been produced by eager and enthusiastic educators. As a result of valuable feedback made possible by viewing numerous productions, the Gallinas continue to learn more about the diverse contingencies which both enhance and sometimes inhibit the scope of amateur and children's theater.

Having served as a music teacher for 9 years, and now entering his 17th year as a public school principal, Michael has had many hands-on opportunities to design and build sets and props for children's theater. His avocation as woodworker and craftsman has contributed to his practical knowledge of materials and construction design. Having achieved a Masters Degree in Music from Trenton State College and a Doctorate in Education from Rutgers University, Michael has extended the knowledge he gained as a practitioner with the theoretical foundations provided by advanced degree programs.

Tom Janssen
Creative Director
Educational Choral Music
Shawnee Press, Inc.

In their efforts to grow and improve as both educators and musicians, Jill and Michael welcome inquiries concerning this book or any performance-related topics. They also enjoy hearing about your various productions and encourage you to share your thoughts with them. You may contact them by addressing your letters to:

Jill & Michael Gallina, P. O. Box 119, Gillette, N. J. 07933

TAKING ADVANTAGE OF YOUR PERFORMANCE HALL

One of the major contributions to the success of your theatrical productions will be the wise and creative use of your performance hall. When you consider the countless hours that go into rehearsals and other preparatory steps, it certainly makes good sense to devote some time to a review of performance hall options. Prior to your first rehearsal, you should have a relatively clear picture of the range of staging and scenery options possible within your performance area. Each production offers unique challenges and equally unique opportunities. What might have worked well for a previous production may not be the best possible approach for your next theatrical undertaking.

The main focus of this chapter will be to assist you in analyzing your performance hall so you can successfully integrate its physical elements into your production. The objective is to mask the imperfections of your facility, while taking full advantage of its unique characteristics.

Because of the wide variety of facilities in which children's theater is performed, this chapter is organized into three sections. The first section deals with elements **common** to most performance areas. The second section deals exclusively with **auditoriums** that have built-in stages and fixed seating. The third and final section deals with **gymnasiums and all-purpose rooms**. Whether you are a director who conducts performances in an exquisite auditorium or one whose stage is only a few feet from cafeteria areas that still smell of the school's daily ration of soggy pizza(!), you will hopefully find suggestions which will help your situation.

COMMON ELEMENTS

Even if you have conducted numerous shows in your performance hall, it makes good sense to re-analyze it for each subsequent production. Prior to taking another careful look at the physical characteristics of the hall, you should become completely conversant with the requirements of each scene of the new production. After this step is completed, it is suggested that you anticipate how the transition from one scene to the next will be handled, keeping in mind any props or sets which might have to be moved or erected. Then the entrances and exits of each performer should be considered so as to provide a sense of fluidity to the performance. Finally, if your production is a musical, the location of the chorus as well as other musicians must be taken into account.

Whether or not you have conducted previous productions in your performance hall, it is still advisable to physically walk through the actual area to be used for each of the scenes. Spend a few quiet moments attempting to visualize each scene. You may be surprised to find that the staging you had envisioned while leisurely reading the script in your living room, might now appear to be unacceptable.

CHAPTER 1
TAKING ADVANTAGE OF YOUR PERFORMANCE HALL

Considering the limited amount of energy you might have to devote to the staging of productions, you may feel the above steps will require too much time; however, in reality, it is time well spent. Directors who mistakenly use rehearsals to discover what does or does not work, waste precious time and eventually promote confusion among the members of the cast. The few moments you commit to the steps noted above will save time and energy, while ultimately contributing to the confidence the students have in you and themselves.

Please do everything within your power to make your production an enjoyable experience for yourself and your students. Early preparation and thorough planning pays high dividends and saves the possible loss of valuable emotional capitol. Stress is a debilitating factor which has negative health implications and limits the ability to perform. It simply makes good sense to devote sufficient time and energy to the planning process.

The suggestions and guidelines contained within will hopefully assist you in engaging in the type of planning that will contribute to the enjoyment and success of your productions.

———

The following questions include some of the elements to consider when analyzing the performance hall. An example of how these elements may influence your staging plans appears after each question.

Question 1
Are there opportunities for performers to make entrances and exits from locations other than the area immediately surrounding the stage?

The director can take advantage of every opportunity to stimulate interest by sending stage action through the audience. For example, in a musical entitled "Lovin' Kindness,"* performers interact and meet in a number of scenes that take place in a park. Each scene involves the entrance of a new group of actors. This production can be enlivened by conducting some of these entrances through the audience. One group can be led down the aisle by a child who is bouncing a basketball. Another group can enter while throwing foam balls back and forth to each other. Using the aisles for group entrances and exits adds another important dimension to your production.

Question 2
Is there a balcony or other raised area that can provide a platform for transitional or mini-scenes?

Quick scene changes can present a significant problem to the director of amateur productions. When too much time is taken between scenes, the audience is distracted and the impact of the production is diminished. If a mini-scene is less than three minutes in duration, it may be worth your while to conduct this scene from a raised area or balcony. Given the short duration of this scene, the audience should not be inconvenienced if they have to turn in a direction

Lovin' Kindness by Michael and Jill Gallina, Copyright © 1992 Shawnee Press, Inc.

away from the main performance area. For example, a scene from a musical involving two young girls who are cousins and located in different countries, read letters they have received from each other aloud. Placing one cousin on stage and the other in a balcony provides the sense of separation, yet underscores the power of their emotional mini-scene which concludes in a duet.

Question 3

If the aisles are large enough, can they be used for some off-stage action?

Surrounding the audience with action – and surrounding the action with audience! – can provide an exciting show stopper. In a musical in which a flood scene is depicted, the actors build a levy by passing sandbags (stuffed paper bags) up onto the stage. They are dressed in rain gear and sing a song about the rising river they are attempting to contain within the levy. As the performers sing, they continue to pass sandbags to the stage. By positioning the actors in the aisles, the audience becomes completely engulfed in the drama of this active scene.

Question 4

Does your performance hall lend itself to audience participation?

Audience involvement can be the spark that transforms unresponsive spectators into interactive and lively participants. While many productions do not include audience participation segments, it is frequently possible for the director to stretch some of the material to include the audience. If, for example, a Santa play calls for him to participate in a classroom scene, why not incorporate the first few rows of the audience into the classroom scene? Save one front seat for Santa and have him join the audience at the appointed moment. When the teacher enters, he or she should address Santa along with the audience members surrounding him. *I have seen this technique employed to the extent that Santa, the teacher, and the audience enjoyed a rollicking repartee which electrified the entire production.*

Question 5

Is it important for the director to be located in an area providing a clear line of sight with performers?

Musical productions have additional requirements that must be addressed.

The answer comes from this experience. *On one occasion, I was faced with the difficult choice of either removing some of the audience seating so I could conduct from the center, or relying on the children to make the musical entrances required by an accompaniment track tape. The children were performing a patriotic partner-song that involved singing, flag waving, and a great deal of movement. Since the students had demonstrated they could make the entrances without my direction, I decided to retain the seating and direct from one side of the performance area. Everything had gone well during rehearsals;*

however, on the day of the performance, we ended up with some "rain on our parade." One group of children slipped behind in their entrances. My position to the side of the performance area prevented me from assisting them with regaining their place in the music. So, our unintentional excursion into avant-garde patriotic music stressed the importance of a central position for the music director! Based on this experience, it becomes evident that performance quality must take precedence over seating for the audience. The director should maintain visual contact with performers, chorus members, musicians, and audio personnel (operating an accompaniment track tape).

Question 6

Will the limitations of your audio equipment restrict the scope of your staging options?

To some extent the response to this question is yes; however, steps can be taken to minimize the negative impact of this type of situation. Because of the feedback loop incurred by poor quality audio systems, it becomes difficult to pick up dialogue taking place away from the relatively restricted area surrounding the microphones. This problem limits performers to the areas within range of the microphones. In order to add an element of variety to the movements of the performers, the director must vigilantly seek opportunities for movement. The following examples are offered as possible options: 1.) Shorter dialogue segments that can be said in a loud voice should be staged away from the microphones; 2.) When the

chorus is singing along with the performers, move the action to another area of the stage; 3.) During scene changes, move microphones to other locations on the stage thereby adding some variety to the positioning of the performers.

FORMAL STAGE WITH FIXED SEATING

Some directors of amateur and children's theater are fortunate to have access to formal performance halls with built-in stages and fixed seating. These individuals appear to have the same opportunities found in professional theaters. Unfortunately, most of these directors do not have the resources to equip or operate their stages in a manner enjoyed by professional production staffs. Whereas professionals have the mechanical means to rapidly change sets, dramatically alter lighting, and create a myriad of costly special effects, most directors of amateur productions must rely on their ingenuity to maximize the basic elements provided by their facilities. The following questions and examples are provided as a means of assisting these directors with capitalizing on the strengths of their somewhat limited, yet potentially fertile, performance halls.

Question 1

Does the stage have wing areas in front of the curtain that can be used for transitional or mini-scenes?

Since the mechanical means to conduct rapid scene changes are usually not available to directors of amateur and children's theater, the following approach may be a viable option. If your stage has wing areas in front of the curtain, both sides of the stage can be used for two different transitional scenes or mini-sets. In the musical entitled "In Quest of Columbus,"* the cabin boys who accompanied Columbus on his first voyage of discovery look upon a scene involving contemporary young explorers in search of Columbus' first landfall. During the course of this production, there occurs an ongoing shift from the cabin boys of the past and their counterparts in the present. By using one of the wings as the location for the cabin boys, a number of time-consuming scene changes can be avoided. The physical space separating the main stage area and the wing of the stage also enhances the transition from the past to the present and vice versa.

Question 2

If there are steps leading up to the stage, can they be incorporated into the production?

Many stages have a dual set of wing steps leading from the audience. Other stages are rimmed with steps that provide easy access to the performance area. If your stage has steps offering a fair amount of square area, consider incorporating them into your staging plans. In scenes where performers are to be depicted in a large outdoor area such as a busy town square, it makes sense to try to spread out the action. This can be done by positioning some of the performers on the steps. Depending on the

* *In Quest of Columbus* by Michael and Jill Gallina, Copyright © 1992 Shawnee Press, Inc.

nature of the scene they may either be standing or sitting. It pays to remember that stage steps are built-in features which frequently can be incorporated into your staging plans.

Question 3

Can you make use of an empty orchestra pit for special effects?

When props, set pieces, or a section of scenery appear by rising out of the pit, the audience is treated to a relatively simple, but dynamic, special effect. The old vaudevillian trick of having countless objects coming out of a trunk can be done easily if an auditorium has an orchestra pit. The front side of the trunk should extend over the edge of the stage. On the audience side of the trunk attach a black skirt which hangs down into the pit. With a person in the pit passing an endless number of large objects through the bottomless trunk, the audience can be treated to an old, yet still quite funny, routine.

(?) **If the pit is very deep, or adequate footing cannot be provided for the actors on the stage side of the trunk, this routine should not be undertaken.**

Question 4

How much room is there between the closed curtain and the front edge of the stage?

If there is sufficient space between the closed curtain and the front edge of the stage, you can conduct some scenes in front of the closed curtain. This will permit additional time to change scenery, while allowing the production to keep moving forward. As evident as it may appear, frequently this simple approach is not used. This technique can also prove to be effective in situations where actors or narrators remain on stage during most or all of the production.

(?) Good judgement must be employed in determining whether sufficient room exists for scenes to take place in front of the curtain. Please be especially mindful of the depth of the orchestra pit and the width of the area between the closed curtain and the edge of the stage.

GYMNASIUMS AND ALL-PURPOSE ROOMS

Many productions are conducted in gymnasiums and all-purpose rooms. This gives directors a wide range of unique challenges. When working in a facility that does not have a built-in stage or fixed seating, you are confronted with contingencies that can limit the scope of your production. On the other hand, some of the elements which seem to be unworkable can be converted into positive contributors to the quality of your production. In the absence of fixed seating, the all-purpose room/gym-style performance hall yields a countless number of creative and interesting options. In order to assist with planning your approach and examining available alternatives, the following questions are provided as a guide to

your decision-making process. Again, since every show has unique needs and structural elements, it is suggested that a full exploration of available components be reviewed for each production.

Question 1
Will a portable stage or raised platform be available ?

If not, the following solution might be considered.

In the absence of a raised performance area, your audience seating options are somewhat limited. Assuming your performers range in height from 3 to 5 feet tall, you cannot have more than eight or nine rows of seating and still expect the audience to see the action. *(Having conducted performances in all-purpose rooms lacking a raised area, I am well aware of the challenges presented by this concern.)* While the following approach cannot be considered a solution, it does provide a number of feasible options.

In order to reduce the number of seats restricting the view of audience members seated farthest from the performance area, consider a variation called "theater-in-the-half-round." Knowing that theater-in-the-round offers even professional performers numerous challenges, this modified approach permits the least restricted view for the audience while still maintaining some directionality to the production. The schematic drawing labeled "Theater-in-the-Half-Round" (Illustration 1-1) contains some of the elements you might consider incorporating into your production set-up. Special details worthy of your attention are:

CHAPTER 1
TAKING ADVANTAGE OF YOUR PERFORMANCE HALL

1. The two radial aisles and the open space in front of the seating area are intentionally included to facilitate the audience's view.

2. A free-standing backdrop (see Chapter 4) is placed 3 to 4 feet from the back wall. Entrances can be made from either side of the backdrop or from some predetermined location along its length.

3. In order to avoid restricting the view of the audience, the conductor should be seated during the production. Accompanying instruments must be low enough to keep sightlines open.

1-1
THEATER-IN-THE-HALF-ROUND

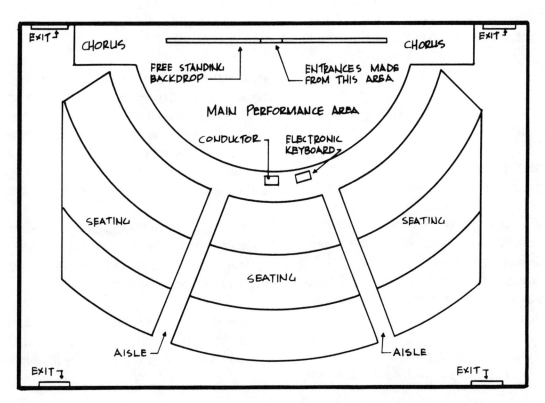

CHAPTER 1
TAKING ADVANTAGE OF YOUR PERFORMANCE HALL

Along with the organizational and seating options noted previously, Chapters 4 and 8 offer some especially useful suggestions for the director electing to use the "theater-in-the-half-round" approach. The portable backdrop support discussed in Chapter 4 not only provides a means to support various components of your backdrop, it also presents opportunities to include free-standing props such as trees and lampposts. The movable partition, also appearing in Chapter 4, should be considered as well. Since the half-round approach to seating places audience members on the sides as well as the front of your performance area, the use of flat props and sets is somewhat limited. The inflatable props discussed in Chapter 8 may very well provide the needed solution to this problem.

Question 2

Can portable choral risers and band risers be used to enhance your production?

Risers used in conjunction with a portable stage present a number of viable alternatives. Not only do risers have utility when used in conjunction with a chorus or band, they can be used to stage mini-scenes (relatively short transitional scenes). When equipped with railings, risers may also provide support for props and sets. Directors can take full advantage of their creativity by locating the risers and the stage in areas that will enhance the effectiveness of their productions.

One of the main reasons for using risers to stage mini-scenes is to provide a raised area which can be seen easily by the audience. Since scene changes are among the greatest challenges of amateur and children's theater, anything which can facilitate this process should be given full consideration. While the audience's attention is focusing on the action in the mini-scene, you have an excellent opportunity to change the set on stage. Depending upon the setting of the mini-scene, the steps of a choral riser section may actually contribute to the illusion the mini-scene is attempting to convey. Examples of this are: a.) In a scene depicting Santa on a rooftop with a chimney propped up at the top of the risers, the steps of the riser simulate the slope of the roof; b.) In a western mountain scene in which boulders and bushes are located on various levels, the risers depict rough terrain.

Because there are so many possible combinations using choral risers in conjunction with a portable stage, a drawing of a standard set-up is included. The schematic drawing labeled "Standard Utilization" (Illustration 1-2) delineates a basic arrangement which can serve as a basis for a number of possible set-ups. Some of the key elements contained within this approach are noted below.

1. In order to provide audience members with the best possible view, the stage has been located on one of the long walls of this rectangular room as opposed to the end of the room (short wall).

2. The steps to the stage are located to the rear rather than the front of the stage. Hidden behind the risers, actors can enter without first being seen by the audience.

3. By placing the choral risers in front of the steps, large props and set pieces (single pieces of scenery) can be accessed easily, yet are not within the view of the audience.

4. The piano is shown to one side of the room; however, if an electronic keyboard is available, it is better to place the keyboard near the conductor and as close to the center as possible.

5. Not only is a center aisle a plus for most performances, it is also a wise consideration in regard to fire safety. The center and side aisles provide excellent opportunities for dramatic, large group entrances. Whenever possible, wide aisles should be incorporated into your set-up and production.

1-2
STANDARD UTILIZATION
GYM/ALL-PURPOSE ROOM STYLE PERFORMANCE AREA

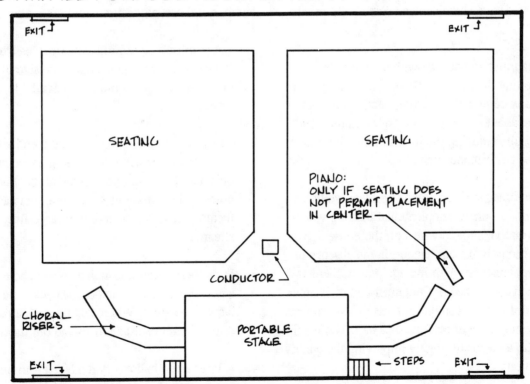

CHAPTER 1
TAKING ADVANTAGE OF YOUR PERFORMANCE HALL

Question 3

Is your performance hall equipped with mercury vapor or another form of very bright, slow start-up lighting fixtures?

If you must work with this type of lighting, you are undoubtedly faced with a real challenge. Not only does the very bright nature of this type of lighting make it difficult to focus light exclusively onto the performance area, the long delay required for re-start makes it impossible to turn them on and off for special effects. While there is no easy solution to the complications presented by this type of lighting, there are steps which can be taken to address this problem.

The first is to familiarize yourself with the multiple switches controlling the lighting. By experimenting with various light bank combinations (some sections on, others off) you may be able to maximize the light illuminating the stage area while reducing the light illuminating the remainder of the performance hall.

Certainly, the ultimate solution to this problem would be to purchase, rent, or borrow supplemental lighting which would permit you to completely turn off the house lights and switch over to portable equipment. In the absence of professional supplementary lighting equipment, there are other steps which can be taken. Contained within Chapter 6, are a number of low-cost suggestions as to how you can improve the lighting in your performance hall. These will provide you with a means of greatly improving the quality of your productions.

Question 4

Do gyms and all-purpose rooms have any advantages over formal auditoriums with fixed seats, a built-in stage, and a curtain?

Without a doubt, gyms and all-purpose rooms have a number of unique advantages which can be used to enhance performances. Some of the suggestions noted here appeared earlier in this chapter. They have been assembled in one location to emphasize the many positive aspects of an open hall performance area. With a bit of ingenuity and creativity, you will be able to incorporate a number of these suggestions into your productions.

1. Large rolling-style props can be wheeled easily into a large open performance hall. The size of these props does not have to be limited to available backstage area.

2. Unlike the formal auditorium, the entire hall can be decorated more easily according to the theme of the program. For example, basketball backboards and other such equipment found in a gym easily lend themselves to the stringing of large flags, banners, and streamers.

3. Some performances, such as plays about team sports and those depicting outdoor scenes, lend themselves to large open areas. When staging such a play, every effort should be made to spread out the action.

4. A large open hall easily lends itself to mini-scenes that can be staged in various areas throughout the perform-

ance hall. Chapter 5 describes how stepladders positioned in different areas in the room can add drama and interest to a production.

(?) **This technique should not be used with young children.**

5. Open performance halls provide natural settings for audience participation segments. In the absence of a formal stage area, the entire audience can be more effectively incorporated into the production.

6. In situations where a number of entire classrooms are involved in a production, the open performance hall is preferred and avoids the confines of the fixed-seat auditorium. With its multiple entrance doors and a large amount of square area, the open hall is a far superior performance option.

7. Unlike the formal auditorium, the open hall quite frequently has exposed internal roof supports which

lend themselves to hanging set pieces and other objects thematically related to the performance.

(?) **Only maintenance personnel should be involved in hanging objects from a high ceiling.**

CONCLUDING REMINDERS

Every performance hall and auditorium has unique attributes that can be harnessed to enhance the quality of your productions. In your role as director you will be called upon to take full advantage of your creative talents in working with the special characteristics and requirements of each play. With a relatively small expenditure of time and energy, you can implement the suggestions contained within this and subsequent chapters to dramatically contribute to the power and impact of your performances.

NOTES

BACKDROPS AND GENERIC SET THEMES

This chapter is devoted to a discussion of the elements that go into the design and fabrication of basic background sets. Along with addressing the artistic implications of the actual set design, there is ample coverage of the practical considerations that go into the making, supporting, and hanging of a background set. Also included within this chapter is a section offering suggestions for ways students can be actively involved in the set design process.

Whether or not the scenery is made under the watchful eye of the director or delegated to someone else, the director is obliged to assume an active role in its conceptualization. The main challenge rests with the director's ability to visualize the requirements of the production. The universal set theme drawings provided within are designed to address this concern.

Since certain themes appear frequently within the literature presented by children's theater groups, this chapter contains drawings of 14 common set themes. It is hoped these drawings can be used in conjunction with a wide range of productions. The drawings of these generic background sets were specifically designed to be projected onto a large wall area and then traced directly onto the material to be used for the backdrop.

Since the director or a volunteer will be tracing the elements contained within the scene onto an acetate sheet for overhead projection, a great deal of control can be exercised over what will be added or excluded. For example, if the play's dialogue makes reference to a split-rail fence, the fence could be added to the drawing prior to tracing the lines. Or, if the distant mountain appearing within the set drawing does not conform to the images needed for the production, clouds could be substituted for the mountain.

CHOOSING THE SET THEME THAT MEETS YOUR NEEDS

The creation of a large backdrop area is, in many ways, similar to the painting of a fairly good-size mural. If you are among the fortunate directors who have the services of an artist who can create a scene on a grand scale, you may choose to use the scenes contained within as a *guide* to the preliminary planning you will conduct with your artist assistant. On the other hand, if the thought of filling a large area with a well-proportioned rendition of a specific setting is a bit disconcerting, perhaps the suggestions in this section will be helpful.

Heavily shaded areas and complicated details have been purposely eliminated from the 14 drawings listed on the following page. This line drawing format will facilitate your ability to first trace the drawing, and then clearly project it onto the material serving as your backdrop. These illustrations can be found at the end of this chapter.

SET THEMES

2-1.   Inner City Neighborhood Store Fronts

2-2.   Barnyard

2-3.   Patriotic Set

2-4.   Inside Santa's Workshop

2-5.   Outdoor North Pole Snow Scene (including Santa's sleigh and house)

2-6.   Inside a Circus Tent

2-7.   Castle Wall and Drawbridge

2-8.   Shipboard Scene (sailing vessel)

2-9.   Evergreen Forest

2-10. Hardwood Forest

2-11. Western Desert

2-12. Tropical Island

2-13. Dickens Era Street Scene

2-14. Interior of a Renaissance Palace Ballroom

Along with the universal sets suggested previously, there are a number of other sources that can serve as templates or patterns for basic sets. The tracing technique explained in the next section can also be used with drawings and photographs obtained from other sources. When using graphic materials not originally intended for set design, the process is more challenging, yet still feasible. The size of the drawing, along with shading and excessive detail, presents some complications. But by restricting the area to be traced to a $3^{3/4}$" x 7" rectangle (these measurements are provided as a basic guide) and by avoiding involvement with minor details, you can successfully use graphic materials obtained from books and magazines. If the graphic materials you have chosen are not similar in size to the rectangle noted above, a photocopy machine with enlargement capabilities can be used to size the drawing to the desired dimensions.

If time and resources permit, you may choose to enhance your set through the addition of three-dimensional details. This can be done by pasting, stapling, or taping various objects onto the set. For example, hanging vines in the tropical island set can be made from thick green synthetic yarn. Cut large leaves out of green crepe paper and at 6-inch to 8-inch intervals knot the yarn around the stems of the leaves. In a scalloped fashion, secure the vines to the backdrop and surrounding areas. Another example involves taping balloons to the circus set. By placing objects such as trees, rocks, and bushes immediately in front of the backdrop, you can augment the three-dimensional illusion created by your set. See Chapter 4 for some suggestions for making free-standing props.

DIRECTIONS FOR MAKING THE SCENE

After having reviewed your play and the staging directions accompanying it, select a set which can be adapted to your requirements. Obtain a black fine-point marker and a clear acetate sheet intended for use with overhead projectors. Place the acetate sheet over the set drawing you wish to duplicate and carefully trace the drawing. Also mark the upper and lower limits of the drawing by tracing the four corners which border the set. These corner markings will prove to be helpful when you are lining up your acetate sheet on the overhead projector.

The tracing you have made can be used to create a backdrop as small as 7 feet high and 12½ feet long or as large as 14 feet high and 28 feet long. Depending upon how you focus the overhead projector, you can obtain a wide range of sizes for the set you have chosen.

In a room that can be darkened, hang the backdrop material (paper or cloth) you have selected. If you have chosen bulletin board paper, you may lightly tape it to the wall. Place the acetate tracing on the overhead and project your set drawing onto the backdrop material. If you would like to make the drawing larger, move the overhead projector farther from the wall. Use the adjustment knob on top of the projector neck to make fine adjustments in focus. The corner markings included on your tracing should now be used to assist you with aligning the tracing to the desired height. By rotating the reflector head on top of the projector, you can properly align the projected set image.

Begin to trace the lines onto your background material.

Use a thick primary-level, soft-lead pencil to trace the lines onto your backdrop. You will need a sturdy stepladder to reach the upper portion of your drawing. This is a lengthy process and depending on the size of your set, a fair amount of time should be allocated for this phase of the project.

(?) **Activities requiring a stepladder should not be done by children. Adults are asked to remember that many ladder accidents occur when individuals try to extend their reach beyond safe limits. Work safely and comfortably. Do not rush. As each section of the drawing is completed and new sections are beyond your reach, move the ladder to the new area. When working on a ladder, always have someone in the room with you.**

After the tracing process is completed, remove the backdrop from the wall and place it on the floor where it can be painted easily. Some people choose to paint as much of the lower portion of it as they can before removing it from the wall. Unless you are experienced in working from a ladder, do not paint the backdrop from the ladder. Do not attempt to re-hang the backdrop while it is still wet.

If you are unable to paint the backdrop in the same room where it will be hung, care should be taken when moving it to another area. If you are using bulletin board paper as the material for your backdrop, you should not tape the various panels together yet. It is easier to handle each panel individually. In order to assist you with recreating the proper hanging order of each panel, carefully number the panels before removing them from the wall.

CHAPTER 2
BACKDROPS AND GENERIC SET THEMES

BASIC BACKDROP MATERIALS

As previously noted, this book is intended as a guide for those who do not have the time or the resources to make professional-style sets. It is for this reason that bulletin board paper is suggested as the primary choice in the selection of backdrop materials. The two standard bulletin board paper widths are 48-inch and 36-inch. If given a choice, the 48-inch width is preferable; however, the 36-inch paper is usually chosen because it is significantly cheaper per roll. If you would like to use your backdrop for subsequent performances, you should consider making it out of cloth. Though it is possible to store and re-use paper backdrops, it is quite difficult to roll and store them without incurring some unsightly wrinkles. If you intend to try to re-use a paper backdrop, be sure to remove all the tape prior to placing it in storage.

One very distinct advantage of bulletin board paper is that it comes in a variety of colors. If your backdrop requires a blue sky, there is no need to paint a large area light blue. Simply use that color paper for the uppermost panel. In the next sections of this chapter, the use and hanging of colored backdrop papers will be discussed.

If you intend to use cloth for your backdrop, be sure you have sufficient funds not only to cover the cost of the yard goods, but also the additional money to buy paint. Unlike bulletin board paper backdrops which accept cheaper school-quality water paints, cloth will require more costly paint. Inform the paint store proprietor of the colors you will need and be sure to explain how the paint will be used. Some paints do not adhere well to cloth and could flake off when the backdrop is rolled and stored.

USING BULLETIN BOARD PAPER FOR YOUR BACKDROP

Since most schools and institutions rarely have room for the storage of theatrical backdrops, sets are often discarded. For this reason, directors may wish to make backdrops out of relatively inexpensive bulletin board paper. This versatile material lends itself to a wide range of applications.

Once completed, a backdrop made from bulletin board paper consists of a number of paper panels taped together. It is strongly suggested that a good quality 2-inch wide masking tape be used to join the paper panels. After the panels have been painted, they are laid painted side down with the edges of the panels placed next to each other and the butt joints are taped. If you are hanging a big backdrop, it makes good sense to have a number of adult helpers.

Panels may either be joined vertically or horizontally. Since bulletin board paper comes in a wide range of colors, this decision may be predicated upon where large areas of similar color will be located. If your set calls for a big blue sky, it is suggested that the panels run horizontally. A set depicting a city skyline consisting of a long line of gray skyscrapers, could be made more easily if the panels were gray and ran vertically. The backdrop should be reinforced with vertical and diagonal strips of duct tape.

Using bulletin board paper backdrops also gives you the option of later affixing – with good-quality double-stick tape – cutouts of various features. Illustration 2-16 demonstrates how horizontal panels can be used to make a desert scene from a variety of colored papers. Use paint to add details and shading.

HANGING THE BACKDROP

If you conduct performances on a formal stage with the capability of flying sets and backdrops, you need not concern yourself with the contents of this section. For performance halls without professionally-styled theater equipment, the suggestions which follow may prove to be quite useful. As a general rule of thumb, it is recommended that backdrops range from 7 to 14 feet in height. In most cases, length is determined by the configuration of your performance hall. The suggestions contained within shall be predicated upon this span of basic height measurements.

The beginning of this section will be devoted to a description of the various methods which can be employed to hang a backdrop. The latter portion will discuss a range of options available when bulletin board paper is selected as backdrop material.

FOUR METHODS FOR FIXED INSTALLATION

There are four different methods used for hanging backdrops: cork strips, wall-mounted cables, battens suspended from the ceiling, and double-stick tape.

The method preferred over all others involves the use of top-quality **cork strips** which have been securely mounted to the wall with *wall anchors*. A securely mounted cork strip allows you to staple your backdrop in place easily and remove it quickly when the production is through. Heavy backdrop materials (all but the lightest of fabrics), are not recommended for cork strip mounting. Please note that cork strips cannot be successfully *glued* to walls. *It seems I have spent the better part of my life picking up hall displays that have fallen as a result of faulty cork strip bonding!*

Wall-mounted cables are also excellent for mounting backdrops. This is a very sturdy system allowing for the hanging of both heavy and light backdrop materials. It is more costly than the cork strip approach and requires additional time to both mount and remove backdrops. The steel cable is securely fastened to the wall with lag bolts which have an eye on the end. The eye of each bolt extends about 2 inches from the wall. The cable is secured to each of the eyes with a turnbuckle permitting tension adjustment of each of the two cables extending horizontally across the back wall of your performance area. This system also allows other set components to be hung in front of the backdrop.

CHAPTER 2
BACKDROPS AND GENERIC SET THEMES

When the backdrop is hung on a **batten suspended from the ceiling**, the director accrues the additional option of creating a quasi-backstage area. Since the backdrop need not be located near a wall, a backstage area can be created. This is the most complicated and involved method. Unless your performance hall closely resembles a formal theater, this approach requires expensive fittings and takes a great deal more time to construct. In many cases this technique is not a viable option since your performance hall may not have beams or other building structural members which lend themselves as a site for the suspension of the batten.

Double-stick tape has been used to hang backdrops, but it is the least desirable method because it is time consuming and labor intensive. Tape does not maintain a reliable bond when affixed to a wall that has been treated with a glossy sealer. Often, the use of double-stick tape prohibits re-use of the backdrop. If you do find a tape which forms a secure bond with the paint, you may unfortunately learn that, upon removal of the backdrop, the paint parts company with the wall as well. Administrators and custodians might take a dim view of this approach!

PORTABLE BACKDROP SUPPORT ALTERNATIVES

If your performances are not regularly scheduled for one specific area, or if installation of the backdrop using one of the previous methods is not permitted in the perform-ance hall, you will have to consider some means of constructing portable or temporary backdrop supports.

By securely fastening (with tape and/or wire) a long batten or pole to the tops of two volleyball stanchions, you can make a temporary backdrop support. The backdrop can be hung from the batten. When this approach is used, the length of the backdrop is restricted to the size of the batten or pole. *If your performance is not in the gym, the volley-ball stanchions cannot be easily moved to another area.*

Chapters 3 and 4 offer suggestions for portable backdrop supports. Chapter 3 discusses standard flat frames which can be wired together to form a backdrop. Chapter 4 offers plans for movable partition supports as well as very compact lightweight supports designed for traveling theater groups. All of these options are free-standing backdrop supports which do not require permanent installation.

PRODUCTIONS REQUIRING MULTIPLE SETS

If you are planning a production requiring multiple sets, there are a number of options to consider. The most basic approach would be to use a neutral light-blue background, and for each set change, bring in free-standing props to create the desired illusion. The mini-scene technique discussed in Chapter 1 can also be used to change the setting without having to use an additional backdrop. The neutral blue backdrop also lends itself for use with the free-standing sets discussed in Chapter 4.

Another way to change multiple sets would be to use your main backdrop to portray the most frequently used setting in the production. Free-standing backdrop supports or the angle set discussed in Chapter 4 could then be placed in front of the backdrop when other scenes take place. An example of this would be a Santa play with many outdoor scenes, and a few scenes taking place in his workshop. The outdoor scene depicting a big light blue snowy sky would serve as the backdrop. When the workshop scene takes place, portable backdrops or the angle set could be moved in front of the main backdrop.

If you do not have a means to hang a backdrop, the following approach may meet your needs. Using three or more of the frames described in Chapter 3, you can make what I refer to as a "flap set." When using this approach, the frames are set up as they appear in Illustration 2-15. The three frames are covered with a secondary backdrop depicting scenes seen the least amount of time. Flaps depicting the main or primary backdrop are then hung in front of the secondary backdrop. At the beginning of the play, the primary backdrop is seen by the audience. When the scene changes, the three primary flaps are draped over the back of the frames thereby exposing the secondary backdrop. If bulletin board paper is used, this change will be a noisy proposition. *I realize this is not ideal, but . . . whoever said we'd be working at the Met?*

CHILDREN AND SET DESIGN

If time permits, it can be quite rewarding to include children in the set design process. For some directors, time restrictions make this an impossibility; however, if a capable volunteer is willing to undertake this task, it can prove to be a fruitful learning experience for the children and a worthwhile addition to the production.

Children's artwork is often exciting and free of inhibitions. Their beautiful creations can make an especially meaningful contribution to your production. As is the case with adult set designers, the children must have a thorough understanding of the production before they can be expected to participate in making a set design.

Using the projection method suggested in earlier sections of this chapter, start by giving children pieces of paper upon which they will draw a 4" x 8" rectangle. Within this rectangle the children should make a pencil drawing of the backdrop they are proposing. Before the children begin, be sure to inform them of all the items or objects that must appear within the set. The children should be told to avoid excessive shading and small involved details. When the pencil and paper drawings are completed, the children should trace their work onto an acetate sheet (as described in previous sections).

The process of selecting student artwork needs to be handled with great care. A thorough understanding of the competition must be established before involving children. It may be possible to select components from designs of several children to be incorporated into the final design. In any case, all must be encouraged to share the excitement they will experience when they see their creation projected in full scale onto a large wall area.

CHAPTER 2
BACKDROPS AND GENERIC SET THEMES

2-1
INNER CITY NEIGHBORHOOD STORE FRONTS

2-2
BARNYARD

2-3
PATRIOTIC SET

2-4
INSIDE SANTA'S WORKSHOP

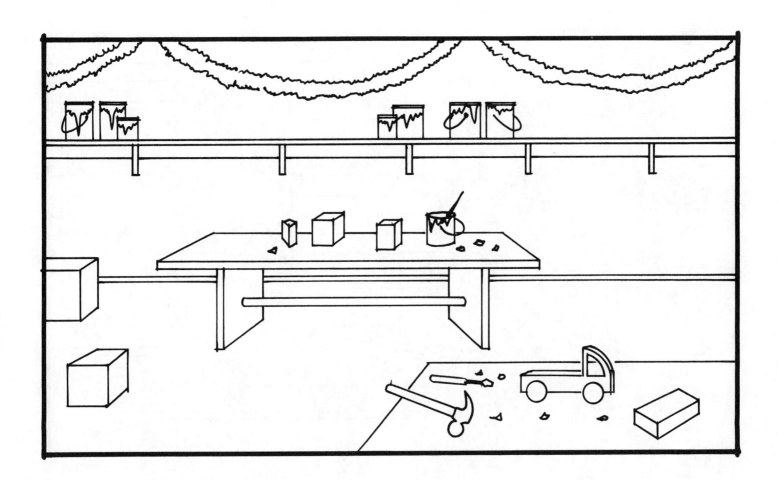

CHAPTER 2
BACKDROPS AND GENERIC SET THEMES

2-5
OUTDOOR NORTH POLE SNOW SCENE

2-6
INSIDE A CIRCUS TENT

2-7
CASTLE WALL AND DRAWBRIDGE

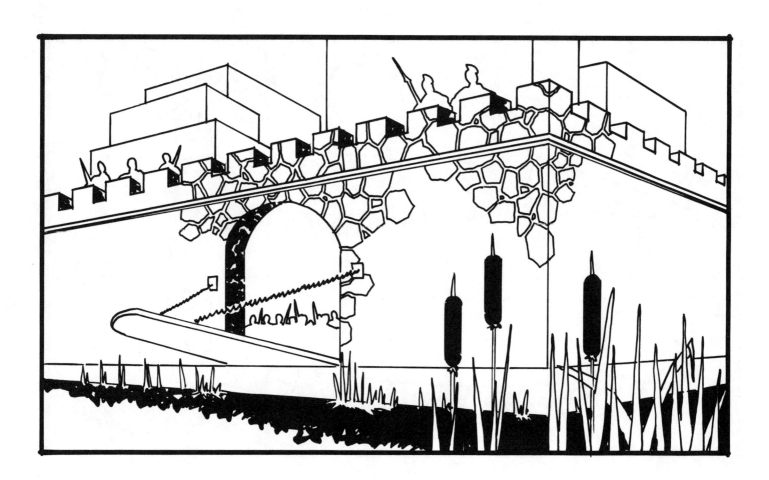

2-8
SHIPBOARD SCENE

2-9
EVERGREEN FOREST

2-10
HARDWOOD FOREST

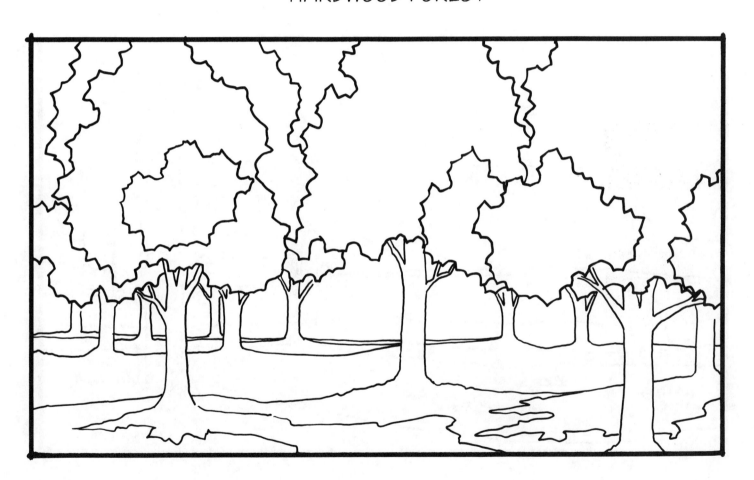

2-11
WESTERN DESERT

2-12
TROPICAL ISLAND

2-13
DICKENS ERA STREET SCENE

2-14
INTERIOR OF A RENAISSANCE BALLROOM

2-15
FLAP SET IN THE PROCESS OF BEING TRANSFORMED
INTO AN INDOOR SCENE

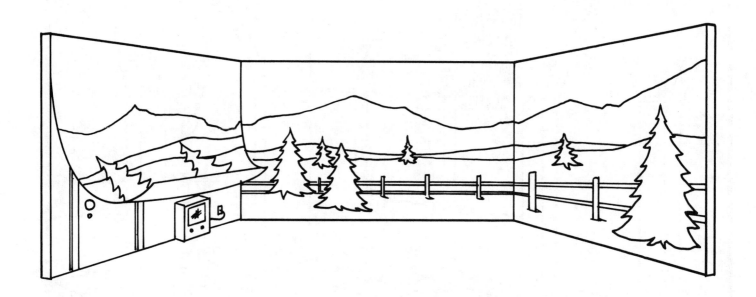

2-16
MULTI-PANEL PAPER BACKDROP

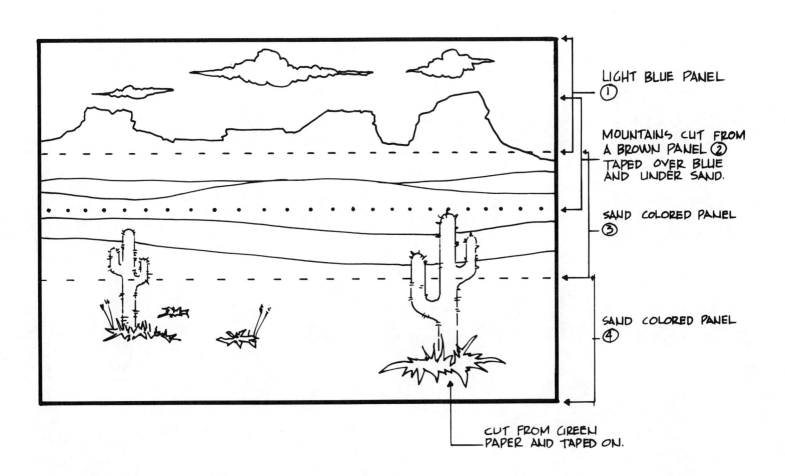

LIGHT BLUE PANEL ①

MOUNTAINS CUT FROM A BROWN PANEL ② TAPED OVER BLUE AND UNDER SAND.

SAND COLORED PANEL ③

SAND COLORED PANEL ④

CUT FROM GREEN PAPER AND TAPED ON.

CHAPTER 2
BACKDROPS AND GENERIC SET THEMES

NOTES

CHAPTER 3

SET CONSTRUCTION BASICS

Chapter 3 deals with the fundamental components which go into the construction of basic flats. Chapter 4 addresses some of the variations achieved by creatively applying the assembly techniques to be explained in the following sections. The flats discussed within were designed to be used alone or in conjunction with a backdrop.

Along with the backdrops discussed in Chapter 2, flats are another fundamental set component which deserve our attention. Unlike the backdrop which is usually large and immobile, flats are movable and flexible stage components. They can be assembled into a wide variety of interesting configurations and imaginative combinations. In order to present ideas that are inexpensive, easy to make, and designed for schools and youth centers, the suggestions contained in this chapter are a slight departure from traditional stagecraft set construction. If, after one trip to the local lumberyard, a group of parents guided by these suggestions can easily build a set that will add a sparkle to your production, then the objective of this book will have been realized.

THE BASIC FLAT

Unlike some of the other ideas offered in this book, this basic flat design was intended to provide a permanent piece of equipment which can be used year after year and for a number of activities other than stage productions. As a director, you may not be interested in uses other than those applying to productions; however, if the availability of funds, maintenance personnel to construct the flats, or storage space is dependent upon the approval of an administrator, you may wish to consider the rationale behind this heavy-duty flat construction. These flats can be used for theatrical sets, school fair booths, puppet theaters, art exhibit frames, and temporary room dividers. Most administrators will approve the expenditure of funds for the construction of a piece of equipment having such long-term, broad-based utility.

Though it may seem unusual to those in professional theater, these flats are constructed from 2" x 4"s. A set of three to five flats should be adequate. Most of you recognize the 2" x 4" as dimensional lumber used to build houses. Why would anyone want to build stage flats from this heavy material? The simple answer is that flats constructed in this manner are strong, easy to fasten together, last a lifetime, and are not extremely heavy. It should be noted that these flats are not used in any situation requiring them to be hung or suspended, nor should they be used to support heavy objects.

If 2" x 4"s are too heavy for your needs, you may consider making them out of 2" x 3"s. In the event money is no object and skilled woodworkers are available to build flats, high-quality traditional pine construction should not be ruled out; however this 2" x 4" design out-lasts and out-performs them all. *Having observed the maintenance crew in my school district throwing my frames onto a truck, I quickly learned to appreciate the value of solid construction!*

FLAT CONSTRUCTION

Illustration 3-1 is a scale drawing of a basic 2" x 4" flat. It is shown resting on its 8-foot base; however, if properly connected to another flat, the 6-foot section can also serve as the base. The two diagonal cross members are not only essential support members, they also provide additional area for the attachment of covering materials. As a result of its inherent strength, this type of flat lends itself to a wide variety of applications.

The structural integrity of this flat relies upon solid corner construction. The corner block or gusset is used to securely fasten the sides to the bottom and top. Merely end-nailing the sides together is not enough. You may either use gussets as described within, or purchase commercial wood fasteners designed for this purpose. Commercial wood fasteners require less time to install, but they do not retain the structural rigidity of the flat as effectively as the plywood gussets. An additional difficulty with wood fasteners is that they occasionally cause splitting especially when the holes in the metal plates end up over a knot or a split in the end of the wood. Gussets, on the other hand, must be cut from 1/4-inch plywood, and require more skill and additional construction time. If time permits, using gussets is the preferred construction method. They are inexpensive, reliable, and if installed properly, quite strong.

3-1
EDGE VIEW OF BASIC FLAT

2x4 OR 2x3 FRAMING

GUSSET

¼" PLYWOOD GUSSET

NOTE: FOR STUDENTS 12 YRS. AND OLDER INCREASE TO 7'

6'

8'

FLAT CONSTRUCTION WITH GUSSETS

Plywood gussets are great for securing the corners of flats. Depending upon how and where your flats will be used, you may elect to employ either single- or double-gusset construction. Illustrations 3-2 and 3-3 provide details for each option. If your flats will not be transported or used for activities other than theatrical productions, you may choose to use a single gusset. Flats that are to be transported and exposed to less than gentle care should be made with double gussets.

This section will provide step-by-step details for making corners with gussets. Assuming you wish to build four flats with double gussets, you will have to cut 32 of them (8 x 4 = 32). This should be approached in an organized manner. Illustration 3-4 provides a diagram of how to lay out your cuts. If laid out according to this plan, you will save time and each gusset will have a 90° edge which will assist you with properly aligning the corners. This plan does not include the gussets needed for the diagonal members of the flat. The gussets used for the diagonal members need not be double.

(?) **Cutting gussets is a task which should be undertaken only by individuals who have experience with power tools.**

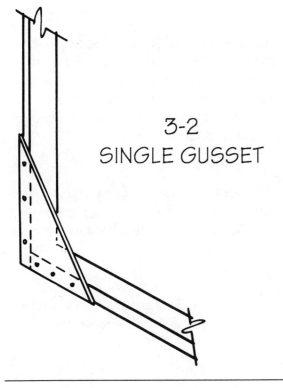

3-2
SINGLE GUSSET

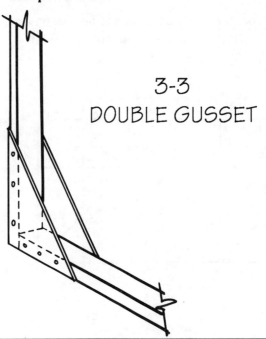

3-3
DOUBLE GUSSET

CHAPTER 3
SET CONSTRUCTION BASICS

Using the cutting pattern delineated in Illustration 3-4, line out a piece of 1/4-inch plywood according to the diagram. This can be done easily by marking 16-inch segments on all sides of a 4' x 8' piece of plywood. By snapping a chalk line on these marks, you can first make the squares of the grid and then follow them with chalk lines for the diagonals. Cut out the 32 gussets and save the scrap piece for gussets that will be used to brace the diagonals.

Follow the construction steps listed below:

Step 1
Cut the sides of the flats (not the diagonals) to the dimensions indicated in Illustration 3-1.

Step 2
Lay the pieces needed to make the sides of one flat on the floor (on edge) in the approximate position indicated by the illustration.

Step 3
Using a carpenter's framing square, square up one of the corners and prepare to attach the first gusset.

Step 4
Use either $1\frac{1}{4}$-inch box nails or no. 6, $1\frac{1}{4}$-inch drywall screws as fasteners. Drywall screws are preferred, but in order to insure against splitting, drywall screws require a pilot hole. Until you are sure the flat is properly squared, use only two fasteners per side and do not drive them completely in. You may need to make some final adjustments prior to securely fastening the gussets to the flat.

Step 5
Using the technique described in Step 3 and Step 4 install the corner gusset which is diagonal to the one that you just completed. Line up the other two corners and use the framing square to determine if any adjustments are required. Drive in the full complement of fasteners once you are satisfied with the fit.

Step 6
If double gussets are desired, ask an assistant to help you turn the flat over on its other edge. Following the steps above, attach the gussets to this side of the flat.

Step 7
Measure for the diagonals and attach them with a single gusset as indicated in Illustration 3-1.

3-4
GUSSET CUTTING PATTERN

GUSSET CUTTING PATTERN
MAKES 32

FLAT CONSTRUCTION WITH WOOD FASTENERS

If the volunteers who will be building your flats are not skilled woodworkers, or if time is a major consideration, you may wish to use commercial wood fasteners. The three main fasteners having utility for the reinforcement of flats are the nail-on plate, the right angle, and the all-purpose anchor. Wood fasteners can be purchased at lumberyards and hardware stores. These fasteners and their three basic applications to flat construction appear in Illustrations 3-5, 3-6, and 3-7. The same basic building steps suggested for the gusset method may be used as a guide for construction. If the holes in the wood fasteners are large enough, use no. 6, $1\frac{1}{4}$-inch drywall screws. Do not purchase the short stubby nails usually used with the fasteners. These nails are too thick and will split the wood when the flats are moved or flexed.

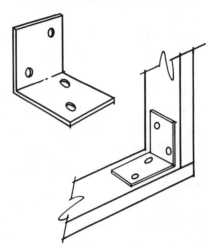

3-6
THE RIGHT ANGLE

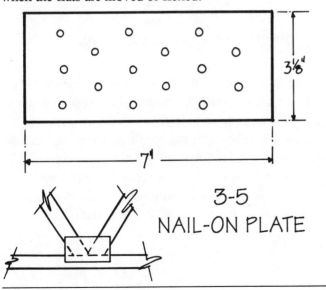

$3\frac{1}{8}"$

$7'$

3-5
NAIL-ON PLATE

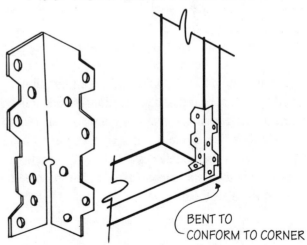

3-7
ALL-PURPOSE ANCHOR

BENT TO CONFORM TO CORNER

CHAPTER 3
SET CONSTRUCTION BASICS

COVERING THE FLAT

As is the case with the backdrop, a wide range of materials may be used to cover the flat. Here again, because of its low cost along with other factors discussed in Chapter 2, bulletin board paper works better than fabric.

Using bulletin board paper as a covering allows you to make cutouts for windows and doors without the need to add other support members. Cloth coverings require additional framing within the flat in order to provide a surface to stretch the material into the desired shape. Paper only requires 2-inch masking tape to reinforce areas around the cutouts. If you have funds to purchase yard goods such as canvas, muslin, burlap, or a cotton blend, be sure to factor into your cost estimate the additional money that may have to be allocated for paints required to adhere to the fabric you have selected. Regardless of the material you have chosen, the covering should be stapled onto the flat. You may staple into all of the non-metal structural members including the gussets.

While it may appear easier to lay the flats down and then staple the covering on, it is better to place the flats in an upright position and, if possible, in the configuration in which they will appear in the production. If done this way, you are able to anticipate what the complete flat configuration will look like and make final adjustments. If using the wire-together method discussed in the next section, you must have the flats in their final configuration before you begin to cover them.

USING YOUR FLATS

Before discussing some of the possible flat configurations available, we must first determine how the flats will be joined together. While there are any number of ways to attach them, two methods provide secure means of attachment. These two options are hinges and bailing wire bindings.

(?) If flats are not securely fastened, or are placed at angles too wide to maintain stability, they can fall and risk injury. Flats placed on the 8-foot side as a base should not be configured at an angle greater than 110°. Flats placed on the 6-foot side as a base should not be configured at an angle exceeding 95°. A flat should never be used alone. The flat construction design appearing in this book was intended for use in configurations requiring at least two flats.

SECURING THE FLATS TOGETHER

Securing flats together with bailing wire has proven to be better than hinges. Though the use of bailing wire binding requires a longer set-up time, it allows for the greatest amount of flexibility. Illustration 3-8 demonstrates how to make bailing wire bindings. Hinges are not as good a choice for securing the flats. The reasons for this are that they are expensive, require more skill to properly install, and inhibit the alternate use of the 8-foot and 6-foot sides as bases.

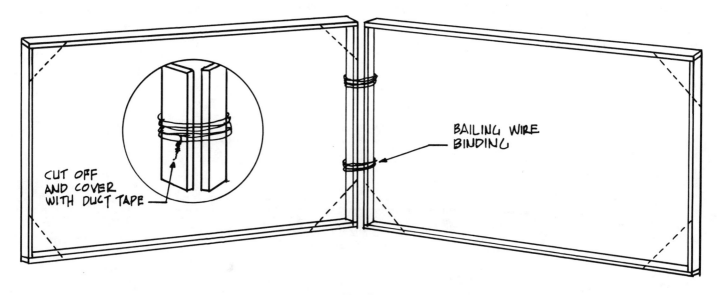

BAILING WIRE BINDING

CUT OFF AND COVER WITH DUCT TAPE

3-8
BAILING WIRE FLAT BINDING

FOR THE PURPOSE OF CLARITY OTHER FLAT
DETAILS HAVE NOT BEEN INCLUDED

(?) **Children should not assist with making the bailing wire bindings. After twisting and cutting off the waste, the twisted end of the wire should be pressed up against the wood frame and the end taped down with duct tape.**

While twisting and cutting off the waste, your adult assistant should turn his or her face away from the area where you are working. When the flats are taken down at the conclusion of your production, the wire should be cut and safely discarded.

CHAPTER 3
SET CONSTRUCTION BASICS

VARIOUS FLAT CONFIGURATIONS

The versatility of these flats will really be appreciated when you see the wide range of possible configurations you can create. Whether used in conjunction with a backdrop or on their own, your options for staging and set design are greatly increased when sections of flats are incorporated into your productions.

The following four pages depict a number of useful flat configurations:

3-9   Three flats can be used to portray an interior space.

3-9
SET ROOM INTERIOR

VIEWED FROM ABOVE →

3-10 When performing without a raised stage in an all-purpose room, four flats can be used to define the performance space while providing a backstage area out of the audience's view.

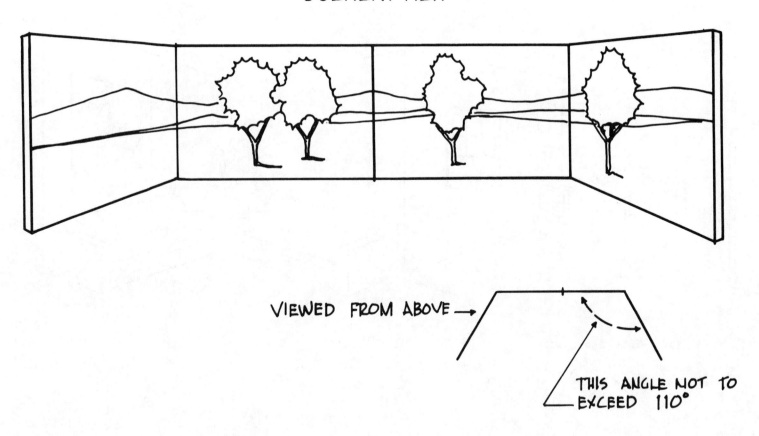

3-10
SCENERY VIEW

VIEWED FROM ABOVE →

THIS ANGLE NOT TO EXCEED 110°

CHAPTER 3
SET CONSTRUCTION BASICS

3-11 A saw-tooth configuration can be used to create the
illusion of two interior rooms within one building, or
interior and exterior spaces adjacent to each other.

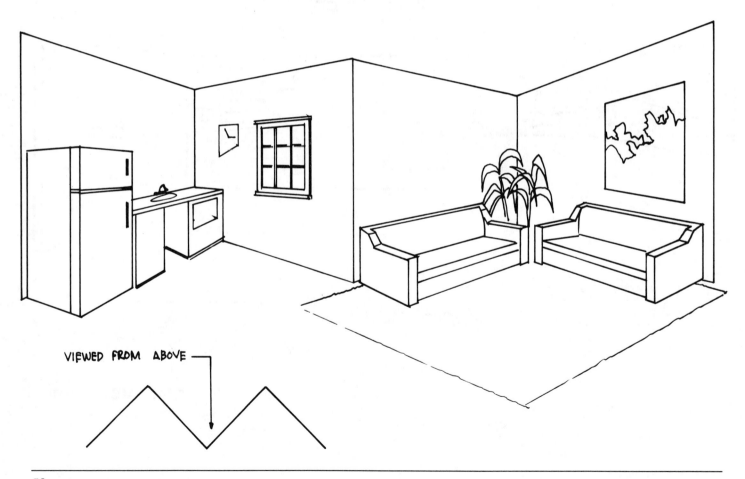

3-11
SET ROOM INTERIOR

VIEWED FROM ABOVE

3-12 When used in front of a backdrop, two separate "V"-shaped configurations can be used to portray two different settings taking place in the same scene. By binding one flat with its 8-foot side on the floor to another flat with its 6-foot side on the floor, you can add interest to the shape of the set.

3-12
INTERIOR/EXTERIOR VIEW

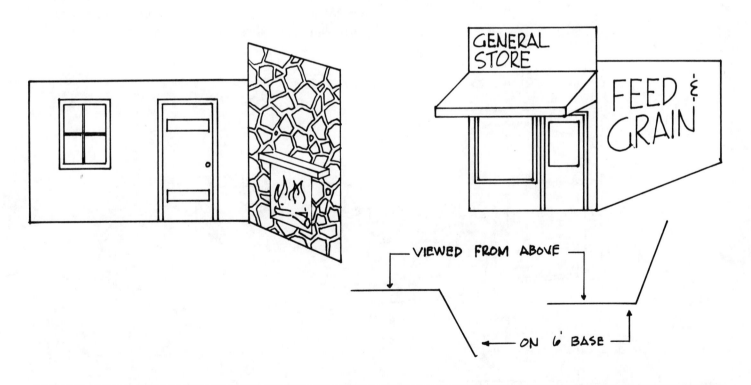

CHAPTER 3
SET CONSTRUCTION BASICS

UNIQUE SHAPES MADE FROM FURRING STRIP FLATS

Furring strips are wonderful for making flats requiring special shapes. Flats made from furring strips are quite flimsy and rarely can be saved, but their special virtue is that furring strips are easy to cut and assemble, plus they are very inexpensive. Since furring strips are made out of inferior quality wood, it is necessary to purchase at least 12 percent more wood than is actually needed. By having some extras on hand, you are able to replace the ones that eventually prove to be too weak. If you intend to purchase furring strips, be sure to obtain them sometime before they are needed for your project. Many lumberyards store this material outdoors where it is exposed to the elements.

(?) Wet wood is not only unpleasant to work with, it can cause tools to fail and thereby result in possible injuries.

The castle depicted in Illustration 3-13 is an example of a furring strip set designed for children in grades K-5. Along with being a colorful three-dimensional set, the midsection of the castle wall lends itself for use as a puppet theater. *With the help of seven parent volunteers at my school, this set was built in approximately 4 to 5 non-stop hours of work!* It is covered with gray bulletin board paper with final details painted on after the set is erected.

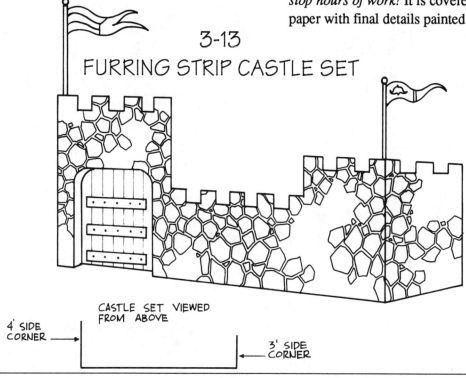

3-13
FURRING STRIP CASTLE SET

CASTLE SET VIEWED FROM ABOVE

4' SIDE CORNER →

← 3' SIDE CORNER

Illustrations 3-14 and 3-15 provide the framing patterns used to construct the castle. You will note that the center section is supported by two side corners (Illustration 3-15) bound to this section with bailing wire. The corners are positioned at 90° to the center section. See Illustration 3-8 for details regarding bailing wire bindings. The three sections of this set (two sides and middle) have a 2" x 4" base positioned flat on the floor. The vertical furring strips fit into a notch which has been cut into the 2" x 4"s. The tops of the castle walls are cut from cardboard or oak tag which has been stretched and stapled in place.

The lumberyard materials required to build the castle set appear below:

1. Thirty furring strips; 3/4" x 2" x 8' (quantity based upon waste due to poor quality).

2. One 2" x 4" x 12' used for base of center section.

3. One 2" x 4" x 8' cut to form both side bases.

4. Two 4' x 8' sheets of 1/4-inch plywood for gussets.

5. Fasteners: no. 6, 3/4-inch screws or 3/4-inch box nails (for gussets); six 2-inch bolts with nuts and washers (see Illustration 3-16); no. 6, $1^{1/2}$-inch screws to fasten furring strips into notch cut in 2" x 4".

3-14
FRAME FOR CASTLE SET

3-15
CASTLE SIDE CORNERS

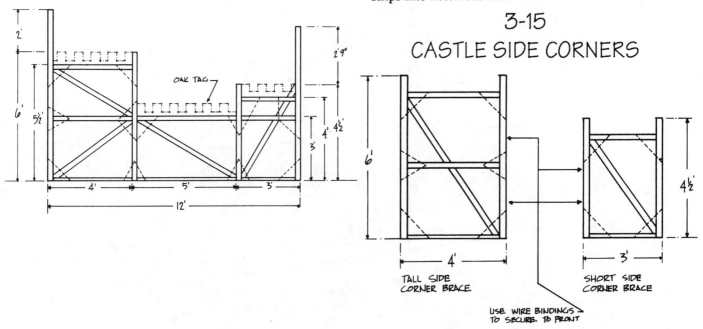

CHAPTER 3
SET CONSTRUCTION BASICS

Illustration 3-16 provides construction details which clarify the joints and connection points used in making furring strip sets. With this information, you or a volunteer can design furring strip sets for your productions. If you plan to custom-design your own sets, begin with a rough sketch which includes approximate measurements. Use graph paper to make a scale drawing of a frame that will support the shape you plan to create. The scale drawing is then used to develop a materials list and also to plan the construction sequence leading to the successful completion of your project.

(?) **Furring strips have very little structural strength. Sets should not exceed 9 feet in height. Supports and uprights (similar to the corner braces for the castle) should be placed at intervals not exceeding 12 inches.**

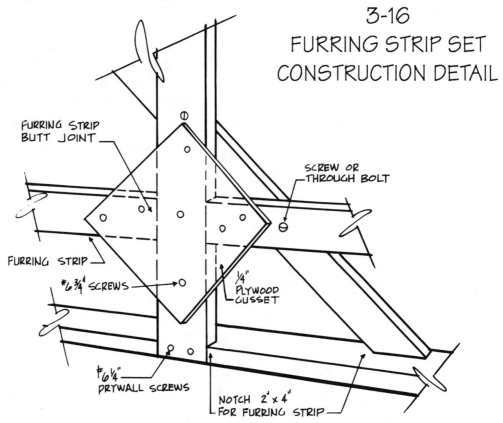

3-16
FURRING STRIP SET
CONSTRUCTION DETAIL

FURRING STRIP
BUTT JOINT

SCREW OR
THROUGH BOLT

FURRING STRIP

#6 ¾" SCREWS

¼"
PLYWOOD
GUSSET

#6 ¼"
DRYWALL SCREWS

NOTCH 2" x 4"
FOR FURRING STRIP

SPECIALTY SETS AND DEVICES

Every director has unique performance and storage needs that occasionally require special sets. Since many of the challenges confronting directors can be associated with the lack of performance and/or storage space, a number of suggestions contained within this chapter will address these concerns. Frequently, inadequate performance areas present an obstacle during the course of the production while inadequate storage areas present a problem at the conclusion of the performance.

When the performance area is limited or restricted, even simple changes become a challenge. Settings such as outdoor scenes may appear well out of reach. Flip sets, trihedron sets (forms a triangle) and free-standing movable partitions are among the options available to the director. This chapter will not only furnish examples of when each option should be considered, it will also provide details for the construction of these viable alternatives.

On a number of occasions, the lack of adequate storage requires the discarding of sets which have taken hours, if not days, to construct. Here again, space is at the root of the problem. The portable backdrop support described and discussed in this chapter is an ideal solution for directors who do not have adequate areas to store set components. Portability, coupled with easy storage in a classroom closet, make this device a must for those who "take their show on the road" or simply from room to room.

PORTABLE BACKDROP SUPPORT

The most basic component of any scene is the backdrop. Within the context of amateur and children's theater, the backdrop is frequently the only element used to convey the desired illusion; therefore it is assumed that provisions would be made for the creation of a backdrop. The portable backdrop support pictured in Illustration 4-1 successfully addresses the two major concerns mentioned in relationship to both performance and storage space. Through the creative use of two or three of these backdrops, the director can maximize available performance space, and at the conclusion of the performance, fold up the backdrop supports and store them in a classroom closet. Another significant feature of this backdrop is that it is very portable. Weighing approximately 6 pounds, and folding into a 3" x 6" x 8' package, several of these backdrops can be transported easily.

While it is possible to get by with only one portable backdrop support, it is advisable to make two or three of them. Each portable backdrop provides an 8' x 7' backdrop area and if three supports are made, you can create backdrop areas either 8-, 16-, or 24-feet in length. The dimensions of these backdrops have been predicated upon the assumption that three of them would be made. Making three at once takes full advantage of the time devoted to each step of the construction process and saves money on materials. It is for this reason the construction details and materials list includes the components required to make three portable backdrop supports.

(?) **Since these portable backdrop supports are designed to be light and portable, care should be taken not to use them to suspend heavy objects or materials. They have been designed to hold up paper (bulletin board paper) and cloth equivalent in weight to bed sheet material.**

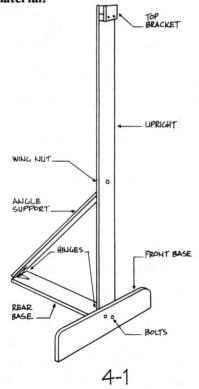

4-1

PORTABLE BACKDROP SUPPORT

MATERIALS LIST FOR THREE PORTABLE BACKDROP SUPPORTS:

1. Six, 8' x 6" (actually $5^{1/2}$") x 3/4" no. 2 pine boards
   a. Three are used to make three uprights and three crosspieces
   b. One for the three front bases
   c. One for the three rear bases
   d. One for the three angle supports

2. Six, 3-inch strap hinges (purchase packets which include screws)

3. Three, $1^{1/2}$-inch bolts with wing nuts

4. Three, 1/2" x 2" mending plates

5. Six, 2-inch carriage bolts with washers and nuts

(?) **The following construction steps require power tools. Individuals who do not have experience with power tools should not attempt to undertake this project. This is not a project for children.**

CONSTRUCTION STEPS FOR THE PORTABLE BACKDROP SUPPORT

See Illustrations 4-2, 4-3, and 4-4 for further construction details.

4-2
PORTABLE BACKDROP SUPPORT

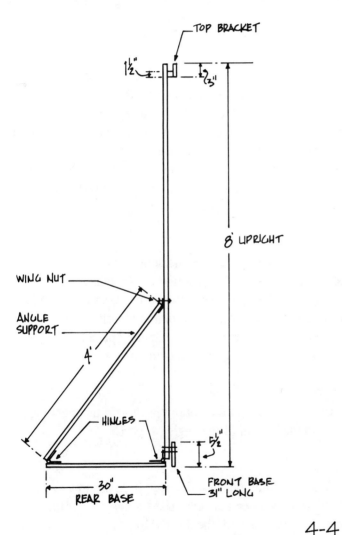

TOP BRACKET

1½"

3"

8' UPRIGHT

WING NUT

ANGLE SUPPORT

4'

HINGES

5½"

30"

REAR BASE

FRONT BASE 31" LONG

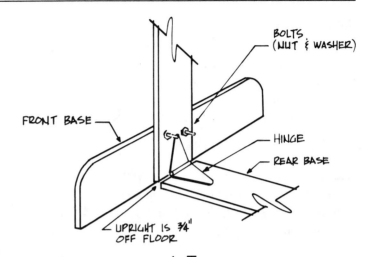

BOLTS (NUT & WASHER)

FRONT BASE

HINGE

REAR BASE

UPRIGHT IS ¾" OFF FLOOR

4-3
DETAILS FOR BACK OF PORTABLE BACKDROP SUPPORTS

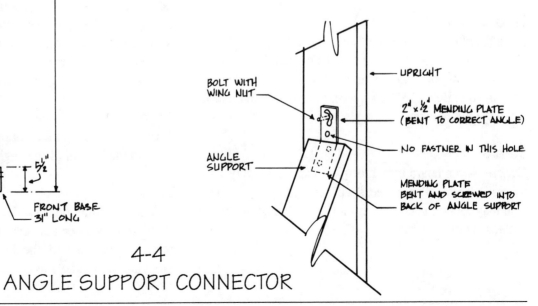

BOLT WITH WING NUT

ANGLE SUPPORT

UPRIGHT

$2" \times \frac{1}{2}"$ MENDING PLATE (BENT TO CORRECT ANGLE)

NO FASTNER IN THIS HOLE

MENDING PLATE BENT AND SCREWED INTO BACK OF ANGLE SUPPORT

4-4
ANGLE SUPPORT CONNECTOR

CHAPTER 4
SPECIALTY SETS AND DEVICES

Step 1

Rip (cut lengthwise) a pine board to obtain one 4" x 8' piece and one 1¼" x 8' piece (approximately 1/4" is lost in the cutting process). It is suggested that the 1¼" x 8' piece be cut from the side of the board with the least number of knots.

Step 2

Repeat the procedure noted in Step 1 with two other 8-foot boards. At the conclusion of this step you will have three uprights and three crosspieces. See Illustration 4-5 for a drawing of the crosspiece.

Step 3

Rip a board to obtain an 4" x 8' piece. Cut this board into three 30-inch lengths which will be used to make three rear bases.

Step 4

Rip a board down the center thereby yielding two 2⅝" x 8' pieces. One of these pieces should be cut into two 48-inch long angle supports. Cut the third 48-inch angle support from the remaining 2⅝" x 8' piece. Save the scrap piece to make the top brackets.

Step 5

Cut one 8-foot board into three pieces approximately 31 inches in length. These pieces will serve as the front bases. You may round the corners as indicated in the drawing, but this is not required.

Step 6

Lay an upright, rear brace, and angle support (in the order noted) flat on the floor and attach a hinge to each of the joints. Be sure to center the angle brace.

Step 7

Place the upright in a vertical position. Attach the front brace to the upright by first marking the center of the upright and the center of the front brace. Place the bottom edge of the front brace on the floor and temporarily clamp the two components together. See Illustration 4-3 before proceeding. Making sure you avoid the hinge, drill two holes to accommodate two 2-inch carriage bolts. Bolt the front brace to the upright.

Step 8

Swing the angle brace up to its approximate support position. The vertical position of the upright may be slightly less than 90°, but it should not exceed this. Once you have determined the approximate position of the upright, bend the center of the mending plate to accommodate the desired angle. See Illustration 4-4.

Step 9

Use screws to attach the bottom portion of the mending plate to the bottom of the angle support.

Step 10

Rest the mending plate on the upright in the area to which it will ultimately be attached. Use the top hole of the mending plate to mark the desired location of the bolt and wing nut. Drill a hole to accommodate this bolt.

Step 11

The top bracket can be made from scrap pieces. It consists of a 1½-inch inner spacer and a 3-inch outer block, each of which is 4 inches long. See Illustration 4-1 and 4-2. Attach the top brace with screws, preferably no. 6, 2-inch drywall screws (be sure to pre-drill).

Step 12

Repeat Steps 6 through 10 to make the other two portable backdrop supports.

Step 13

Six inches from the end of each crosspiece, slightly round the corners to facilitate their fit into the top brackets.

Step 14

Use sand paper to slightly round all the edges thereby reducing the possibility of splinters.

Step 15

Depending on the quality of the pine and the humidity of the area where the supports will be stored, it may be advisable to coat the supports with a wood sealer.

4-5
TWO PORTABLE SUPPORTS
WITH CROSSPIECE IN PLACE

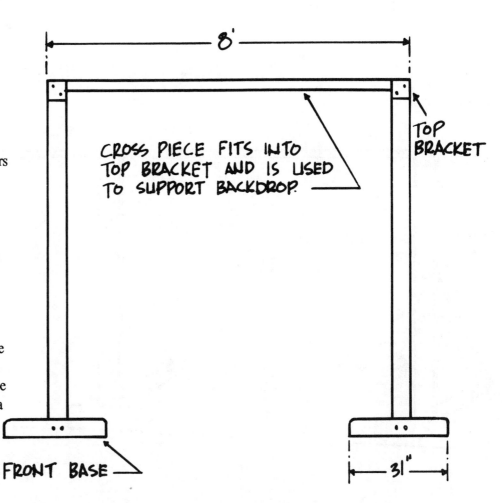

CROSS PIECE FITS INTO TOP BRACKET AND IS USED TO SUPPORT BACKDROP.

TOP BRACKET

FRONT BASE

8'

31"

CHAPTER 4
SPECIALTY SETS AND DEVICES

USING YOUR PORTABLE BACKDROP SUPPORTS

As indicated in Illustrations 4-5 and 4-6, the crosspieces can be supported end-to-end by placing them in the top brackets. Another useful approach is to put the middle of a crosspiece in the top bracket thereby forming a "T" support. When used in the "T" configuration, the crosspiece should be taped to the top bracket. The "T" configuration offers a number of set options. Three "T"s could be used to form three walls of a room. On the other hand, by leaving space between the "T"s, you have created areas

4-6
END-TO-END CONFIGURATION

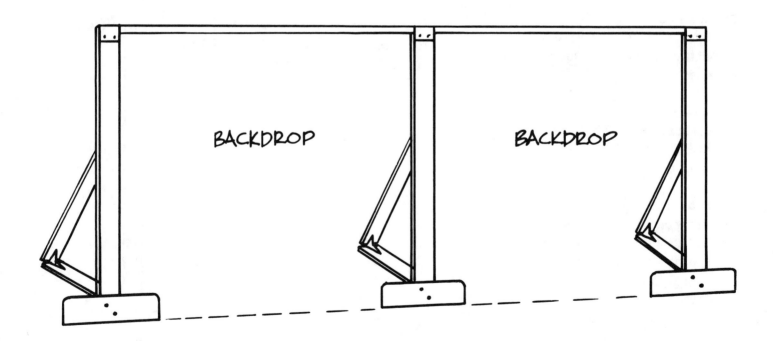

which can be used for entrances by your performers. See Illustration 4-7.

If you install one crosspiece in the normal position of two supports (see Illustration 4-5), and tape an additional support to the midsection of these supports, you can create a puppet theater. Hang a border from the top crosspiece and a skirt from the middle crosspiece. When transporting your puppet theater, simply roll the cloth border and skirt around the crosspieces to which they are attached.

When used with specially made crosspieces, the backdrop

4-7
PORTABLE BACKDROP USED IN A "T" CONFIGURATION

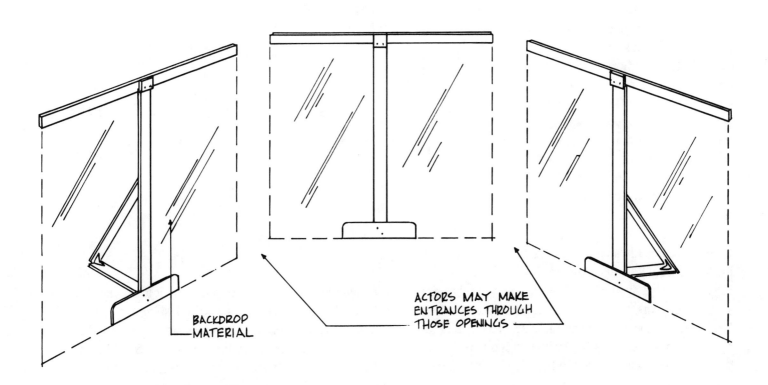

BACKDROP MATERIAL

ACTORS MAY MAKE ENTRANCES THROUGH THOSE OPENINGS

supports can be successfully used to create a number of free-standing props. They can be used to make trees, lampposts and other useful props. As long as you do not use the supports to suspend heavy objects or thick materials, their utility is unlimited. Enjoy being imaginative.

MOVABLE PARTITION SET

If flexibility is a key factor in the staging of your next production, consider using movable partition sets. A play containing multiple scenes or a show calling for entrances from a number of different directions requires flexibility which can be achieved with this type of approach. Since the movable partition set consists of separate, self-supporting flats, the configuration of these mini-backdrops can be changed during the course of the production.

If you have already decided to construct the heavy-duty flats discussed in Chapter 3, you will have available to you the structures that serve as the framework for movable partition sets. As seen in Illustration 4-8, the movable partition set is a 6' x 8', 2" x 4" flat which has been stabilized with end supports. These supports permit the partition to be independently posi-

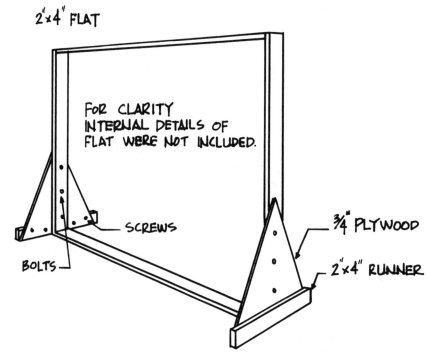

4-8
MOVABLE PARTITION SET

2'x4" FLAT

FOR CLARITY
INTERNAL DETAILS OF
FLAT WERE NOT INCLUDED.

SCREWS

BOLTS

3/4" PLYWOOD

2"x4" RUNNER

tioned without the need for attachment to another flat. Since the end supports have been designed in such a manner as to permit easy removal, they greatly enhance the use and flexibility of the 2" x 4" flat. See Chapter 3 (section labeled "Various Flat Configurations") for a discussion of the numerous uses for the 2" x 4" flat.

4-9A
CONSTRUCTION DETAIL OF END SUPPORT

4-9B

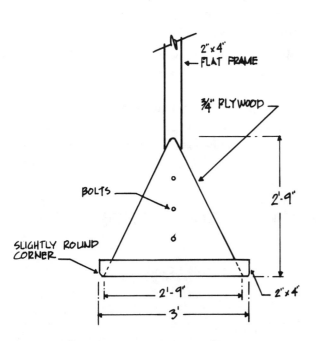

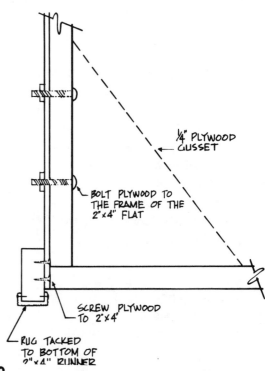

MOVABLE PARTITION CONSTRUCTION DETAILS

Illustrations 4-9 A and 4-9 B provide the details required to construct the movable partition end supports. The following construction steps also include a list of materials and fasteners.

Step 1

Cut two 3/4-inch pieces of plywood into triangles that are 2' 9" at the base and have a height of 2' 9".

Step 2

Cut two 2" x 4"s into 3-foot lengths for the runners. The bottom corners of the runners should be slightly rounded.

Step 3

Cut two 3-foot long strips of indoor/outdoor carpet and fasten them to the bottom of the runners. Note the method of attachment suggested in Illustration 4-9 B. In place of the carpet, you may choose to use four 2½-inch socket-style casters. They can be installed near the end of each runner.

Step 4

Use sixteen no. 8, 2-inch deck screws (eight per side) to fasten the plywood to the runners. Be sure to drill pilot holes for the screws.

Step 5

Firmly clamp the end supports to the end of the flat and leave approximately 3/4-inch clearance off the floor. Drill holes to accommodate six 1/4" x 3"-long round head bolts (slotted for a screwdriver). Purchase washers and nuts along with the bolts. Since the gussets make for tight quarters in the corners where the bolts will be installed, the slotted end of the bolt should be in the interior of the flat. It is easier to reach in with a screwdriver than with a wrench.

(?) In order to prevent injury, cover the exposed ends of the bolts with tape.

USING YOUR MOVABLE PARTITION SETS

As the name implies, these sets are designed to be moved during the course of the production. They are to be gently slid (or rolled if on casters) into position. When moving these partitions, force should not be applied higher than the top of the triangle. Pushing or pulling above this point could cause the partition to fall over. The repositioning of these partitions is not a task for lower elementary children. If your cast includes only this age group, you might recruit fifth or sixth graders to assume the responsibility of moving the partitions.

These partitions possess a unique attribute in that they can display a different scene on each side. By rotating the flat, a different scene can be exposed to the audience. Illustration 4-10 provides a group of overhead views depicting

4-10
CONFIGURATIONS FOR MOVABLE PARTITION SETS

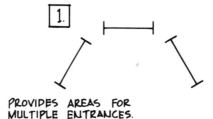

PROVIDES AREAS FOR MULTIPLE ENTRANCES.

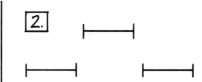

MINI-SCENE AREA CAN BE USED FOR FLASHBACK OR DOUBLE SCENES THAT OCCUR IN ONE TIME FRAME.

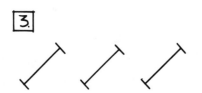

LENDS ITSELF TO LARGE GROUP ENTRANCES INVOLVING MOVEMENT AND DANCE.

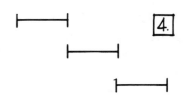

CITY STREET SCENES OR LOST IN THE WOODS TYPE OF SCENE THAT INVOLVE BACK-AND-FORTH, IN-AND-OUT MOVEMENTS.

four different configurations created with three 2" x 4" flats equipped with end supports. It is interesting to note that each of the four configurations conceivably could be used within the context of one production. The fourth configuration is the most interesting since it lends itself to any number of creative applications. For example: 1.) characters lost in the woods wander around each of the partitions; 2.) multiple entrances can be made from four locations around the partitions; 3.) the partitions could be used in a street scene to represent a row of dwellings.

Since each partition has a triangular support on each end, a resourceful director can take advantage of this feature. For example, if a forest scene is chosen, the triangles can serve as a means of propping up bushes; or when used in conjunction with a city street scene, the triangles can be used to support a cutout depicting steps leading into the houses. These are just a couple of examples of how a potential minus can be converted into a plus. Covering exposed support pieces with scenery reduces the risk of cast members bumping into them.

THE FLIP SET

One of the set designs reflecting techniques used in professional theatrical productions is the flip set. This set requires more time to construct and is usually built to accommodate the needs of a particular production. Although this can be a more costly approach, by using materials such as 2" x 3" lumber, furring strips and bulletin board paper, expenses can be kept in the moderate range. If you are planning a production that will be a significant commitment in time and effort, this type of set may be a justifiable expenditure.

The flip set remains on stage during the entire production and is turned around (not actually flipped) to alternately portray two of the major scene requirements. In many situations, the flip set is the most expeditious means of depicting the interior and exterior view of the same structure. The selection of a flip set need not always be predicated upon this particular application. The main criteria is whether the silhouette for one scene can also be used to portray the setting for a second scene when turned around. You can easily explore your options by making a small scale cutout of your first scene. Flip it over and see if you can use it to support the set details required for your second scene. With a little imagination, you may be pleasantly surprised to find that the silhouette of the flip side can be incorporated into your second scene.

(?) If you are seriously contemplating building a flip set, there are two considerations that must be taken into account. If a flip set exceeds 7 feet in height, it becomes increasingly difficult to rotate. Also, it should be noted that a flip set cannot be rotated by elementary age children. Adults will be needed to rotate the set. The number of people needed is based upon the height and size of the set.

A thematic setting frequently used in children's plays involves scenes that take place in and around a cabin or small house. Themes related to Abraham Lincoln, Johnny Appleseed, Thanksgiving, western settings and even

CHAPTER 4
SPECIALTY SETS AND DEVICES

Santa's workshop typically require the basic indoor/ outdoor approach. Illustrations 4-11 and 4-12 offer a typical flip set. This particular set can have a brown bulletin board paper exterior (Illustration 4-11) with dark brown or black highlights. The stone chimney could be

gray or a light shade of brown. The interior walls (Illustration 4-12) could be covered with a light colored earth-tone paper or could be left uncovered revealing the structural members of the frame. Three-dimensional objects which are either tacked to or leaned against the set

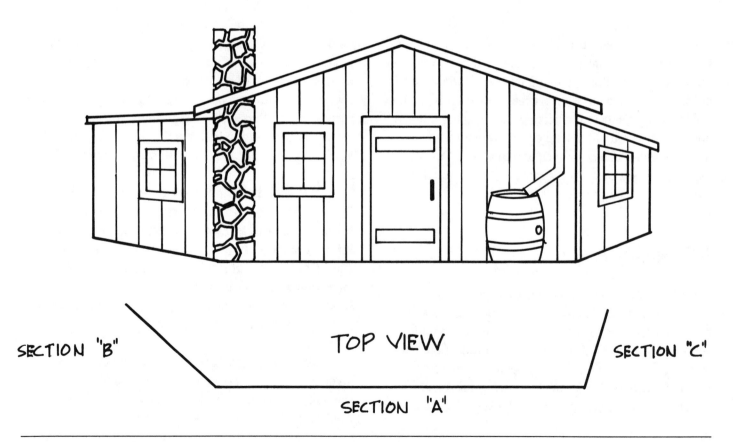

4-11
CABIN EXTERIOR

SECTION "B"   TOP VIEW   SECTION "C"

SECTION "A"

add a great deal to the impact of the scene. You can paint the rain barrel on or place one in front. Objects such as animal furs and farm tools can also be added to the exterior of this set. The interior scene can be enlivened with real objects including clothing hanging from hooks along with other three-dimensional objects such as a broom or a lantern placed by the wall. As long as you do not attempt to hang heavy objects from the frame, there is actually no limit to the range of opportunities presented by this set.

The cabin pictured in Illustration 4-11 has vertical siding. If a log cabin is desired, the same frame is used except horizontal logs with circular log ends are drawn onto the

4-12
CABIN INTERIOR

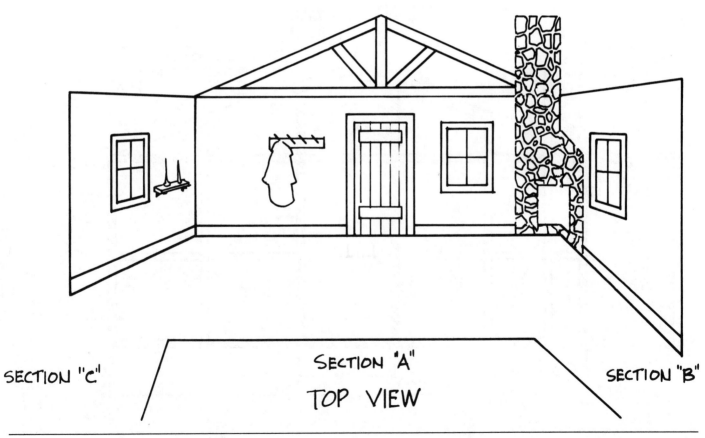

SECTION "C"   SECTION "A"   SECTION "B"

TOP VIEW

bulletin board paper. With a little bit of creativity, this one basic flip set framework could be used to depict a wide range of settings. For example, Santa's workshop is needed frequently for holiday plays. By converting the drawing of the cabin to portray a small cottage with red shutters and horizontal siding, the flip set takes on a whole new character. By adding icicles and a snow covered roof, the setting needs only a red and white North Pole to be complete.

BUILDING THE FLIP SET

Illustrations 4-13 and 4-14 provide a description of the materials and the construction details required to build the cabin flip set. The main feature of the frame is that it is made from 2" x 3" lumber. Furring strips, while not included for structural strength, have been added to provide a surface on which to staple the bulletin board

4-13
FRONT OF CABIN

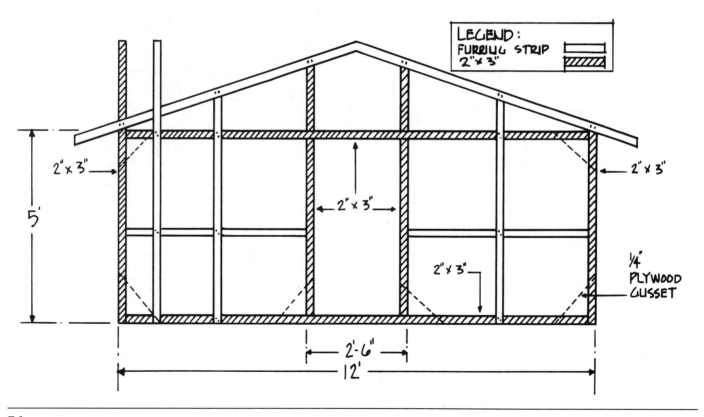

paper. The vertical furring strips are notched into the 2" x 3" lumber. Refer to Chapter 3, Illustration 3-16 for specific details. Even though the less costly plywood gussets are depicted in the drawing, please note this type of construction lends itself to the use of the time-saving wood fasteners discussed in Chapter 3; Illustrations 3-5, 3-6, 3-7. Be sure to purchase wood fasteners designed for use with 2" x 3" lumber. Screws are recommended. It always makes good sense to drill pilot holes for the screws.

4-14
CABIN SIDES

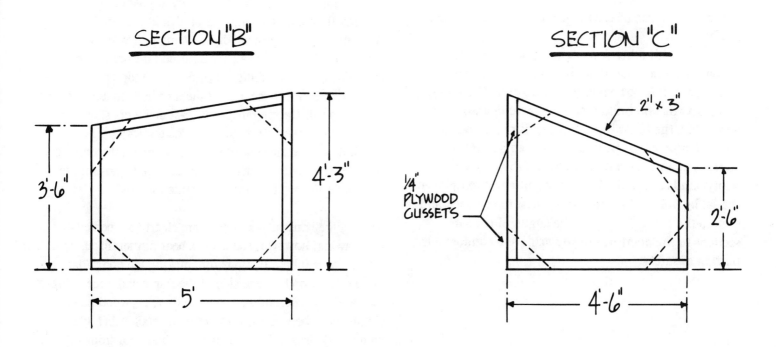

SECTION "B"

SECTION "C"

3'-6"

4'-3"

5'

2" x 3"

¼" PLYWOOD GUSSETS

2'-6"

4'-6"

Since it is unlikely your lumberyard will carry a straight 2" x 3" x 12', it will be necessary to scarf (join end to end) two 2" x 3" boards to form the top and bottom horizontal pieces. If you have an experienced woodworker as your assistant, he or she will be aware of the many ways this can be done. If time is a problem, they may be scarfed together with two nail-on plates (see Illustration 3-5) fastened to the top and bottom of both boards.

Illustration 4-14 gives the dimensions and construction details for the "B" and "C" side sections. Since the angular orientation of the sides to the main section "A" are not altered when the set is rotated, the wire hinge shown in Illustration 3-8 can be used to join the sections together.

(?) **As with other free-standing sets, the side support sections should not be placed at too wide an angle. Since it is not possible to determine the stability of the set you will build (you may include a working door, etc.), the following safety test is recommended: 1.) With only adults present, set the angles of the side sections in a position that appears stable. 2.) With many hands available for support, attempt to tip over the set by pulling the top portion first to the back and then to the front. 3.) Adjust the angles of the side sections to the point where you achieve a comfortable margin of safety.**

BUILDING A WORKING DOOR

Occasionally, scenery-making responsibilities are complicated by productions requiring the actors to make entrances through a door that opens and closes. While there are staging options that make it possible for you to get around this requirement, the entrances have greater impact when staged as originally intended.

If one of your set construction volunteers possesses even minimal woodworking skills, he or she will be able to make the basic working door shown in Illustration 4-15. One essential component required by any working door is a sturdy frame. It is for this reason that 2" x 3" or 2" x 4" construction is suggested. Unlike some professionally made sets, this door does have a raised threshold. In order to minimize the possibility of tripping, the top corners of the bottom board in the area of the threshold should be well-rounded. During rehearsals, cast members should be reminded that they must step over the threshold. The threshold can be eliminated if the area around the entrance is reinforced and braced; however, this approach is more expensive and requires more construction time.

Most of the construction details are clearly delineated on the drawing; however, some steps bear further discussion. Be sure to build the frame before making the door. Place a piece of plywood on one side of the frame and trace along the interior portion of the frame onto the plywood panel. Cut the door between 1/8- to 1/4-inch smaller than the guide mark drawn. In order to restrict the door from swinging beyond the radius provided by the hinges, be sure to attach a stop block on the side of the frame oppo-

4-15
WORKING DOOR CONSTRUCTION DETAIL

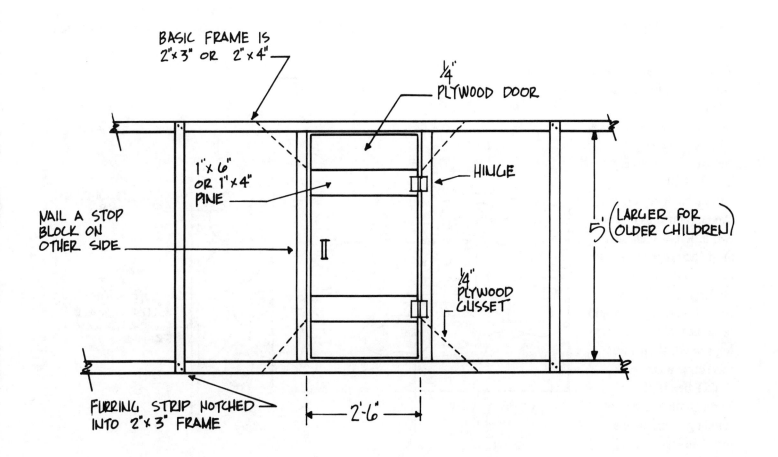

BASIC FRAME IS
2"×3" OR 2"×4"

¼"
PLYWOOD DOOR

1"×6"
OR 1"×4"
PINE

HINGE

NAIL A STOP
BLOCK ON
OTHER SIDE

5' (LARGER FOR
OLDER CHILDREN)

¼"
PLYWOOD
GUSSET

FURRING STRIP NOTCHED
INTO 2"×3" FRAME

2'-6"

site the hinges. The pine reinforcement boards are attached to the door by driving the screws through the plywood and into the pine boards on the other side. As with any theater prop, do not allow cast members to play with the door or subject it to harsh use.

THE ANGLE SET

When performance space, money, and time are a problem, the angle set should be considered as a prime option for set design. It is relatively light and, like the previously described flip set, it can be rotated to reveal two different scenes. If more than two scenes are required, the flap set approach shown in Chapter 2, Illustration 2-15 should be considered. By designing a window area into this set, you can gain further flexibility. Through the use of freestanding props such as furniture and other objects, these props and

the scene in the window can be changed thereby indicating the action is taking place in a different setting. Admittedly this is a low budget approach to scene changes, however, it does provide a setting with a fair amount of credibility.

Illustration 4-16 provides a perspective drawing of an angle set. One side of the set has an angled upper portion

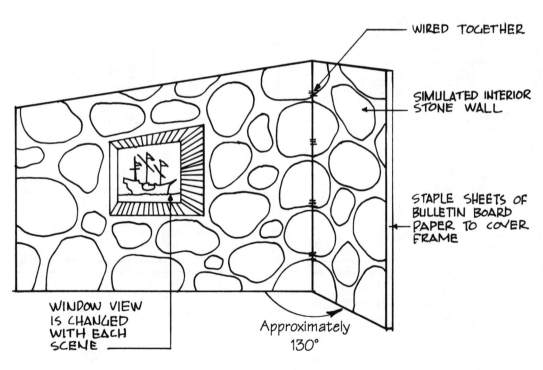

4-16
ANGLE SET

WIRED TOGETHER

SIMULATED INTERIOR STONE WALL

STAPLE SHEETS OF BULLETIN BOARD PAPER TO COVER FRAME

WINDOW VIEW IS CHANGED WITH EACH SCENE

Approximately 130°

in order to promote the perception of depth. Illustration 4-17 provides the construction details required to build this set. Because of the need to save money and weight, this set is constructed entirely of furring strips, 1/4-inch plywood, and bulletin board paper. Here again the two flat frames are joined together with the wire hinge described in Illustration 3-8. As with other free-standing flats, care should be taken not to exceed the angle recommended in Illustration 4-16.

4-17
CONSTRUCTION DETAILS FOR ANGLE SET

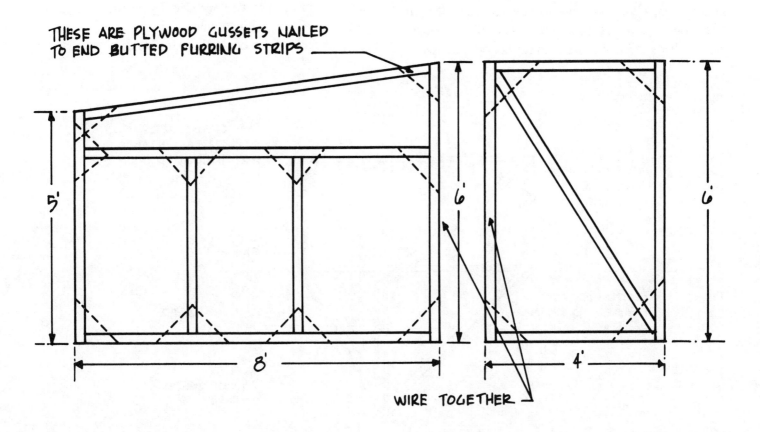

THESE ARE PLYWOOD GUSSETS NAILED TO END BUTTED FURRING STRIPS

WIRE TOGETHER

CHAPTER 4
SPECIALTY SETS AND DEVICES

TRIHEDRON SET

A trihedron is a triangular cake-slice shaped set consisting of three faces which can be alternately exposed to the audience. Whether you choose to use one unit, a pair, or a set of them, they offer the director a unique array of creative options. Illustration 4-18 is an overhead perspective drawing of a trihedron set consisting of three 2" x 4" flats wired together. See Chapter 3, Illustration 3-1 for construction details for this type of flat. In each corner of the trihedron, a 3/4-inch plywood base has been bolted to the bottom. Because of the weight of this unit, it is recommended that casters be attached to each plywood base. If

adults will be assigned the task of rotating and moving the trihedron, you may replace the casters with indoor/out-door-style carpeting. When 2" x 4" flats are placed into a trihedron, they can be separated easily and used again for other purposes.

When performance space is at a premium, a single trihedron unit may be an ideal approach. Since there is space inside each unit, performers can even make entrances and exits through a door cut in the bulletin board paper. You can maximize use of the three sides by incorporating a flap set orientation (Illustration 2-15) into your plan. The flap paper panels can be turned to the inside of the triangle.

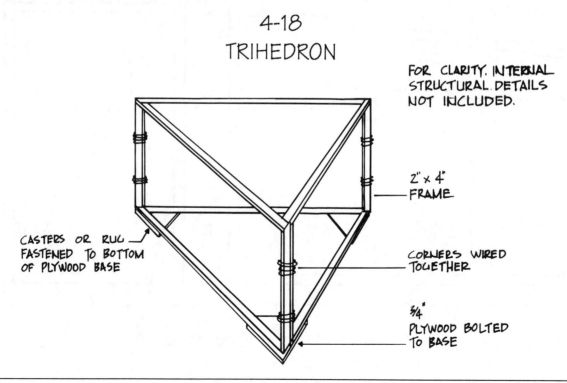

4-18
TRIHEDRON

FOR CLARITY, INTERNAL STRUCTURAL DETAILS NOT INCLUDED.

2" x 4" FRAME

CORNERS WIRED TOGETHER

3/4" PLYWOOD BOLTED TO BASE

CASTERS OR RUG FASTENED TO BOTTOM OF PLYWOOD BASE

A pair of trihedrons can provide you with an endless spectrum of intriguing possibilities. Illustration 4-19 presents just a few of the many options. When more than one unit is used, the director has the means to sculpt the performance area into a shape that conforms to his or her visualization of the scene. This three-dimensional sculp- ture can be altered continually during the course of the production; however, multiple units require a great deal of square area. If the multiple trihedron approach is a strong consideration for your next production, be sure you have sufficient performance space before you begin to build the units.

4-19
TRIHEDRON CONFIGURATIONS

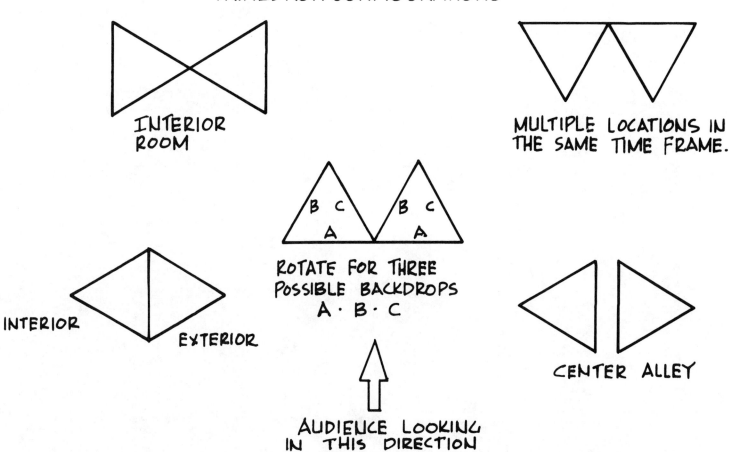

INTERIOR ROOM

MULTIPLE LOCATIONS IN THE SAME TIME FRAME.

INTERIOR

EXTERIOR

ROTATE FOR THREE POSSIBLE BACKDROPS A · B · C

AUDIENCE LOOKING IN THIS DIRECTION

CENTER ALLEY

NOTES

CHAPTER 5

COMMON ITEMS/UNCOMMON USES

In the process of organizing my notes for this chapter, I recalled an expression used by one of my undergraduate psychology professors. His phrase, "functional fixedness," describes an individual's inability to visualize the use of an object for anything other than its intended purpose. Whether this expression is a real psychological term or just something he invented does not, for the purposes of this chapter, diminish its usefulness. In fact, overcoming "functional fixedness" is what this chapter is all about. Given the limited resources available to many directors, they can ill afford to suffer from "functional fixedness."

Every object in the school or institutional environment must be perceived as possibly having some application in a theatrical production. The numerous examples provided in this chapter will hopefully assist you in conceptualizing many alternate uses for a wide range of objects which are readily available to you.

For example, music stands do a great job of holding our music and they can also be used to fulfill a number of unique production requirements. Whether used to support a wide range of small props or enlisted to serve as mailbox posts, music stands have utility well beyond the function for which they were designed. If a script calls for a rolling set, why spend money and time building something from scratch when a rolling chair rack can easily be converted to this purpose? Why devote hours to the construction of a

street vendor's cart when a utility cart or mobile audio-visual table can quickly be modified to meet this need?

Quite simply, our schools, auditoriums, and youth centers are filled with objects that can easily be used as time-saving props and set enhancements. In order to save you time in identifying these objects, this chapter has been divided into four sections. Each of these sections represents a categorical area to facilitate your search. The four sections are:

- •OBJECTS USED TO SUPPORT PROPS
- •OBJECTS THAT PORTRAY MOVEMENT
- •THREE-DIMENSIONAL OBJECTS
- •SUPPORTS FOR SET PIECES AND BACKDROPS

Since a number of the items discussed within have multiple uses, their various attributes will be noted in more than one section.

In order to identify objects that may have application within your productions, it is not necessary to read all four sections. For example, for a play taking place in a wooded setting with free-standing trees, simply consult the section entitled OBJECTS USED TO SUPPORT PROPS. When a scene calls for a school bus to come to a stop on stage, read the section labeled OBJECTS THAT PORTRAY MOVEMENT. First identify your needs, then read only the sections devoted to your main area of interest.

CHAPTER 5
COMMON ITEMS/UNCOMMON USES

By using the suggestions in this chapter as a guide, you can better employ your own creative talents to identify accessible and useful objects. Having cast off all vestiges of "functional fixedness," you will be better equipped to enhance the quality of your productions while gaining more time for rehearsals.

OBJECTS USED TO SUPPORT PROPS

Many of the props used in amateur productions are flat representations of real objects. If a scene calls for a free-standing wishing well, the director would most likely choose to create a flat representation of this object. Volunteers responsible for creating flat props might want to invest time and money in devising a means for them to stand, but by wiring (bailing wire) or taping flat props to items such as student chairs and desks, a great deal of time, effort and money can be saved.

Student Desks and Chairs

Student desks and chairs are readily accessible and easily handled prop supports. Props may be secured to student furniture with tape, string, or bailing wire. If additional support is needed, rulers, pointers, or yard sticks can be taped onto the sides of desks or the backs of chairs. When using a chair as a prop support, the back of the chair is usually faced toward the audience.

Application 1

Illustration 5-1 demonstrates how a wishing well prop can be supported by a student desk. The roof area is

supported by furring strips that have been wired or taped to the legs of the desk. The front of the well is painted onto bulletin board paper or cardboard. Furring strips are secured to the desk with wire or tape and the front of the prop is stapled to them.

Application 2

Frequently there will be a need for a special chair such as a king's throne. In this case, it is suggested that an adult-style straight-back chair be used and a piece of cardboard cut and painted to look like the high back of a throne chair. The high back is then taped to the back of the chair. If further authenticity is desired, a short decorative skirt can be taped around the front and side edges of the chair.

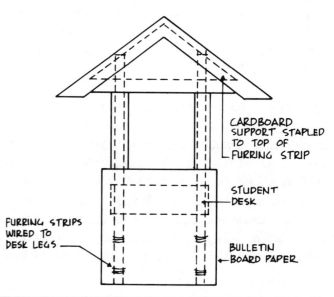

5-1

STUDENT DESKS AND CHAIRS

CARDBOARD SUPPORT STAPLED TO TOP OF FURRING STRIP

STUDENT DESK

BULLETIN BOARD PAPER

FURRING STRIPS WIRED TO DESK LEGS

5-2
MUSIC STANDS

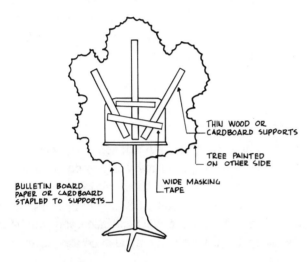

THIN WOOD OR
CARDBOARD SUPPORTS

TREE PAINTED
ON OTHER SIDE

BULLETIN BOARD
PAPER OR CARDBOARD
STAPLED TO SUPPORTS

WIDE MASKING
TAPE

Music Stands

While folding music stands occasionally can be used as prop supports, the stands discussed here are standard orchestral and band music stands. Given their stability, rotating top, and adjustable height, music stands present numerous options to directors. Another significant feature is that most stands can be raised to approximately 4' 10" in height. Listed here are a few of the many ways music stands may be used.

Application 1

Any object found on a post can be easily affixed to the top of a music stand. Objects such as mailboxes, birdhouses, traffic signs, and candy dispensing machines (gum ball, etc.) can be portrayed successfully with the assistance of a music stand.

Application 2

Bushes and small trees may be depicted by taping or wiring foliage to a music stand. Extend the top of the stand to the desired height. The actual shape of the tree is formed with bulletin board paper or cardboard. See Illustration 5-2.

Stepladders

Since stepladders come in a number of different heights, they provide a wide variety of options to directors. They are high and stable, thereby making them primary choices for the support of larger props. The triangular shape presented by a stepladder also lends itself to some unique applications.

Application 1

The triangular shape of the stepladders makes them a natural choice for supporting free-standing evergreens. A group of stepladders of varying heights can be transformed into an eye-catching pine forest. Bulletin board paper should be cut to shape and then taped to the triangular side of the ladder. If you use green paper, details may be added with paint or marker.

Application 2

If your production calls for an Indian tepee, you can add some interesting effects if a tall stepladder is used to create the tepee. Use brown bulletin board paper and cut it to shape. Details may be added with paint, marker, or cutouts pasted onto the surface of the tepee. Entrances and exits can be made from the tepee if a flap door is cut in the bottom of the paper.

Application 3

A sense of depth can be added to a forest or jungle scene by adding some free-standing foliage. Ladders ranging in size from the two-step to the multi-step versions can be used to support flats simulating various foliage configurations. Contribute to the perception of depth by positioning them at different distances from the backdrop.

Easels and Chart Stands

Art easels, chart stands, and paper pad easels are most useful in situations involving smaller productions. If your presentation will go on the road or simply from room to room, consider using one or more of these items as set and prop supports. Easels are very useful because they are free-standing and can support painted versions of various objects. As with other flats, objects can be painted on bulletin board paper and then secured to the easel with tape.

Application 1

Chart stands used in early childhood and lower elementary classrooms are especially useful and versatile. They stand in a perfectly vertical position (most easels lean back) and the attachment rings on the top bar permit displays to be either removed or flipped over.

Application 2

Easels provide a high display area which includes a tray upon which non-rectangular items may be placed. If you are conducting a play on nutrition and wish to display various cut-out shapes representing different food groups, an easel will serve the purpose quite well.

Traffic Cones

Since most physical education teachers have included traffic cones in their regular inventory of equipment, these items are usually available in most school settings. Stable, short, and sturdy, traffic cones offer a number of unique options. They not only provide a surface upon which items can be taped, the center hole may also be used to support taller items.

Application 1

When many small free-standing props are required, the traffic cone is an ideal choice. If surface rocks and boulders are to appear in a scene such as a desert setting, traffic cones can easily support numerous free-standing, relatively small objects. Simply tape a painting of a rock onto the traffic cone or tape wrinkled brown bulletin board paper to each cone.

Application 2

The traffic cone, unlike other items in this list, may be called upon to play itself. If you are performing a program with a circus theme, brightly decorated cones would be a welcomed sight. Decorate them with a construction paper conical sleeve which has been taped over the cone. The sleeve can be painted brightly and covered with glitter.

Application 3
Look for opportunities to incorporate cones into settings in which they would normally appear. Scenes involving city streets, construction sites, and lines of people are occasions when traffic cones can be used in real-life settings. Traffic cones are easily handled real-life props which add depth and contribute to the illusion you are trying to create.

Tripod Projection Screens
Tripod projection screens are excellent prop supports; however, as a result of their weight, they are not easy to move. Because of their tendency to fold when being moved, children should not be permitted to handle them. Once the base is opened and the screen portion is rolled up and in the vertical position, projection screens are tall and relatively stable.

Application 1
Illustration 5-3 displays the screen in the position noted in the previous paragraph. While in this position, the outline of a lamppost or other tall object can be taped to the side facing the audience.

Application 2
The cylindrical shape of the upper portion of the screen lends itself for use as a support for a cactus

plant or other similarly shaped prop. See Illustration 5-4. The shorter arm of the cactus is supported by a piece of cardboard taped to the screen cylinder.

Application 3
In shipboard scenes or any other setting requiring a cylindrical object (smokestack, ship's mast, etc.) the tripod projection screen's shape makes it a natural. It is suggested that you tape a large cylinder (made from bulletin board paper) around the smaller cylinder housing the screen.

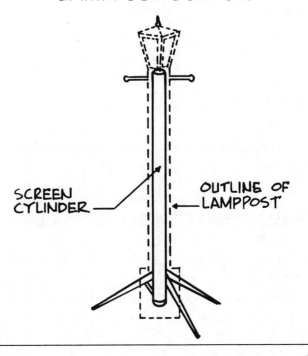

5-3
TRIPOD PROJECTION SCREEN:
LAMPPOST SUPPORT

SCREEN CYLINDER

OUTLINE OF LAMPPOST

5-4
TRIPOD PROJECTION SCREEN: CACTUS SUPPORT

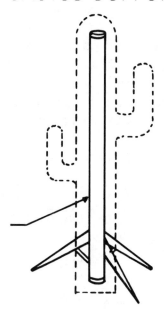

(?) **Some tripod projection screens cannot be configured as noted in Illustrations 5-3 and 5-4. If your screen cannot be positioned easily as illustrated, do not try to force it into this configuration.**

OBJECTS THAT PORTRAY MOVEMENT

One of the greatest difficulties for directors may be the portrayal of moving objects. Usually, when something has to move on stage, it involves wheels of some type. Since casters and wheels are quite expensive and time-consuming to install, we frequently avoid, eliminate, or work around any settings with this requirement. As a result of this missing element, otherwise excellent productions fall a bit short of the mark. Schools and other institutions are filled with items that not only have wheels, but also provide sturdy frames upon which to mount sets and props. This section of Chapter 5 is devoted to an exploration of some noteworthy applications of these common, yet rarely used items.

Rolling Chair Racks (Chair Trucks)

One of the most useful pieces of equipment found in the school and institutional environment is the rack used to store folding chairs. Since rolling chair racks (chair trucks) exist in almost every institution, they present some very attractive alternatives. These racks range in size from approximately 60 inches to 125 inches long and are usually constructed of heavy-duty metal frames. As a result of their narrow wheelbase, the racks are difficult to steer and can become unstable if heavy items are mounted too high on the frame.

Chair/coat storage racks are the type used to provide an overhead frame for hanging coats. Consisting of a 5- to 6-foot frame, the chair/coat truck offers a limitless array of opportunities. While only one possible use for the chair/coat rack will be noted within this chapter, directors are reminded that this item can be applied creatively to a wide spectrum of staging requirements.

> **(?)** 1. Some folding chair racks have only a narrow rail on each side. Children should not be permitted on this type of chair rack.
>
> 2. As a result of the narrow wheelbase, chair racks should be moved slowly.
>
> 3. A child should not be allowed on a rolling chair cart if the cart will be pushed toward the edge of a raised performance area or be used in the vicinity of an incline.

Application 1

A number of Santa plays depict him as either preparing to take off or having just landed in his sleigh. By fastening a cutout of a sleigh to the side of a rolling cart, you can successfully incorporate this basic illusion into your production. The cart need not be pushed across the entire stage. If the sleigh is depicted as arriving, just the front portion of the cart would be pushed into the audience's view. See Illustration 5-5.

5-5
CHAIR RACK: SANTA'S SLEIGH

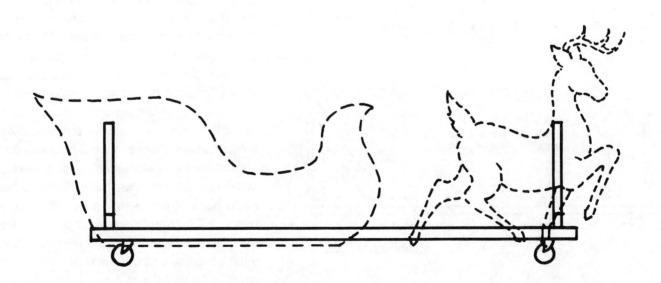

CHAPTER 5
COMMON ITEMS/UNCOMMON USES

Application 2

If your script calls for a train pulling into a station or a large boat pulling up to a dock, the logical approach is to have the station (stylized portion of the station) move to the train and in the case of the boat, the dock move to it. Even though the audience is well aware of what is happening, the end result is a somewhat primitive, yet effective, illusion. These rolling sets can be created very easily if a chair rack is used to provide the framework. Illustration 5-6 provides the required details for the construction of a dock.

5-7
CHAIR/COAT RACK: SCHOOL BUS

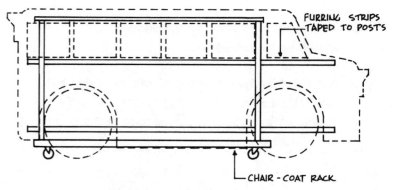

FURRING STRIPS TAPED TO POSTS

CHAIR - COAT RACK

Application 3

Some plays portray the arrival and/or the departure of children on a school bus. With the aid of a chair/coat rack you can create a moving bus. Because a number of children will be involved, they should not actually ride on the bus (chair/coat rack). As the bus (flat of bus attached to chair rack) is rolled onto the stage, the children will be visible through the windows, thereby giving the appearance they are riding in it. Since they are not actually riding on the cart, the children should be directed to walk along the side not seen by the audience. When the bus stops, they can walk out in front of the bus as if they were getting off. See Illustration 5-7 for further details. In order to extend the rack to the size needed for the school bus, it will be necessary to tape two horizontal furring strips to the uprights of the rack.

5-6
CHAIR RACK: DOCK

CARDBOARD AND BULLETIN BOARD PAPER SIMULATE PILINGS AND DECK

CHAIR RACK

Carts

Schools and institutions are filled with carts of every conceivable size, shape, and configuration. Cafeteria carts, audio/visual aids carts, library carts, custodial carts, computer carts, and many, many more. All of these carts have potential for inclusion in theatrical productions thereby saving time, money, and energy. The following suggestions are just a few examples of the hundreds of useful theatrical applications that can be addressed through the use of readily available carts.

Item 1: TV/Video Cart

If the script calls for the entrance of a large creature, for example a dinosaur, consider using a high TV/video cart to support a cutout of this monster. Also, the creature can be represented by an inflatable rendition which has been taped to the cart. See Chapter 8 for more information regarding inflatables. Illustration 5-8 provides an example of how an inflatable can be taped to a cart. When the dinosaur is wheeled about the stage, care should be taken to not reveal the cart that is on one side of the inflatable or cutout. If the lights are dimmed and the child assigned to wheel the cart is dressed in dark clothing, the illusion may prove to be more effective.

Item 2: Standard Equipment Cart

City street scenes really come alive when carts are incorporated into the setting. Standard equipment carts lend themselves to this application very well. Their approximate measurements are 30 inches high, 24 inches wide, and 32 inches long. The sides can be covered with bulletin board paper and details depict-

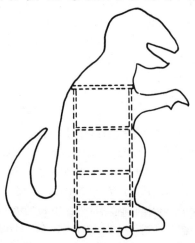

5-8
HIGH TV VIDEO CART:
INFLATABLE DINOSAUR

ing a variety of street vendor-style pushcarts can be painted on. By attaching a beach or large golf umbrella to one side of the cart, you can simulate a hot dog stand. The cart's large front wheels can be painted on the side, or if time permits, cut from cardboard and secured to the internal shelving of the cart.

Item 3: Carts in Tandem

Productions involving circus themes can benefit from the addition of rolling animal cages. A group of two or three carts can be employed to depict the cages used by lion tamers. The carts can be linked together and pulled out onto the stage. Here again, cover the sides with bulletin board paper and paint on lions. The bars of the cage can be black strips of paper pasted over the figures of the lions.

CHAPTER 5
COMMON ITEMS/UNCOMMON USES

Wheeled Utility Equipment

A number of useful wheeled utility items can be readily found in the institutional setting. In view of the extensive variety of wheeled items found in most work environments, the following suggested uses will be limited to four pieces of equipment. Hopefully, the examples stated below will provide you with some ideas for making better use of the wheel-mounted equipment that is available in your particular setting.

Item 1: Wheeled Trash Barrel

Illustration 5-8 demonstrates how an inflatable creature can be taped to one side of a TV/video cart. While it is relatively easy to add motion to your creature using this approach, you are limited to a left/right range of motion. If time permits, you can provide multi-directional movement to your inflatable monster by taping the open bottom of the creature over the top of a clean, wheel-mounted trash barrel. This can be done by sealing all but the bottom portion of the inflatable creature. Since the interior of this inflatable must pass over the large circumference upper portion of the barrel, be sure your inflatable is baggy enough to accommodate this step in the process. Once the inflatable has been pulled down over the barrel, seal the bottom with duct tape. See Chapter 8 for more details regarding the construction of inflatables.

Item 2: Rolling Step Stool

If the script calls for a small animal such as a raccoon to run across the performance area, this can be done easily by taping a cutout of a raccoon to the side of a rolling step stool (known as a KIK Step Stool). Frequently, this type of stool can be found in libraries and stockrooms. With the aid of a string, a child can pull this two-dimensional animal across the stage.

Item 3: Gym Scooter

Here again, if the movement of a small animal is needed. This suggestion affords an additional degree of flexibility. If you can obtain a stuffed version of the animal noted in the script, you can use a gym scooter to create the desired illusion. Since the gym scooter is a low-wheeled platform approximately 12" x 12" in size, it can support a variety of objects easily. By taping the stuffed animal to the scooter platform, you can provide a wide range of multi-directional movement.

Item 4: Utility Ball Rack

When the script calls for a large dog, donkey or pony-sized animal (not a character with a speaking part) to move within a scene, the director may use a child in a costume to portray the animal or consider making a rolling prop. Rather than making a costly and time-consuming costume, you can build this prop. As a result of its width (9 inches) and height (40 inches), the gym ball rack lends itself quite well to this purpose. By adding a head and covering the sides of the cart with cloth or paper, you will create an animal that can be lead about the stage effortlessly by one of the performers. See Illustration 5-9 for further details.

5-9
UTILITY BALL RACK: PONY

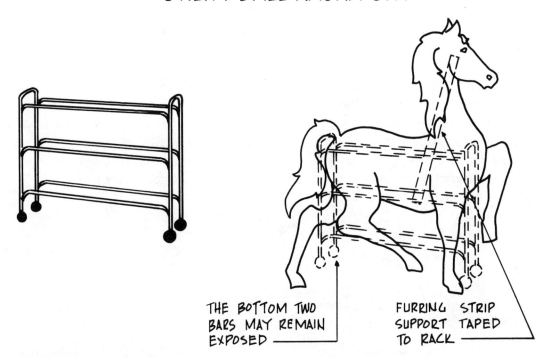

THE BOTTOM TWO BARS MAY REMAIN EXPOSED ——

FURRING STRIP SUPPORT TAPED TO RACK

THREE-DIMENSIONAL PROPS

When the real thing is not available, too heavy, or simply too difficult to manage, you can create a prop from items found in your immediate environment. The items noted in this section provide a basic structural framework for making props that can be tailored to your purposes. Even though you may not have access to all of the items following, you can use these suggestions to guide your creative application of equipment accessible to you.

Stepladders

As a result of its availability and stability, the stepladder again appears under one of the four major headings contained within this chapter. If you are in need of a three-dimensional, triangle-shaped object, the stepladder should be one of your prime candidates. Since stepladders come in various sizes, they can portray objects as big as a roof, or as small as a pup tent.

CHAPTER 5
COMMON ITEMS/UNCOMMON USES

Application 1
Scenes depicting Santa on a rooftop can be given a special touch by creating a pitched roof with a window permitting entrances and exits from the house. Peter Pan- or Mary Poppins-style productions also may call for rooftop scenes. See Illustration 5-10 for further details. If entrances will be made through the window, slit open the sides and bottom of the lower window pane. As noted in the drawing, only two sides of the roof are covered with bulletin board paper. The 2" x 4" border (painted black) is used to signify the edges of the flat roof upon which the characters will stand. As shown in the illustration, the peak of the roof is formed by two 2" x 4" boards that have been

secured to the top step of each ladder. Two furring strips serve as a means of supporting the bulletin board paper used to represent the shingled roof. The treetops depicted in the scene should be reflective of the season (winter = branches, summer = green).

Application 2
If you are planning a production involving a summer camp group or a scouting group, you may have a need for pup tent-style props. In order to create these objects, use small stepladders covered with cloth or bulletin board paper. Here again, a crosspiece will be needed for the peak of the pup tent.

5-10
STEPLADDERS: SUPPORT ROOFTOP

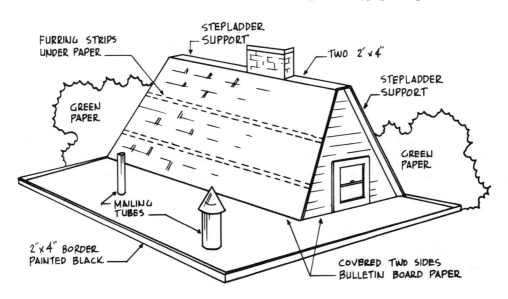

Project Tables

Project tables range in size from 6 feet to approximately 10 feet in length. They can be as narrow as 24 inches or as broad as 42 inches. These tables are found in most institutional settings. The folding variety is portable and offers the greatest range of applications.

Application 1

With the addition of a partial skirt or border, project tables can be dressed up to resemble a number of different pieces of furniture. If the script calls for a massive wooden table or a bulky-style desk, you can depict them by using paper to represent the required features. Illustration 5-11 provides two suggestions for accomplishing this.

Application 2

When a full skirt is added to one or more project tables, you can create a number of objects. One of the most frequently required objects is the store display case or counter. Whether your scene requires a display case from a modern department store or an old country store, you can create a skirt that conveys the desired illusion.

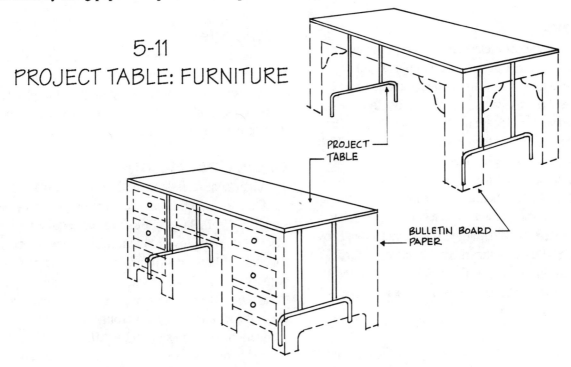

5-11
PROJECT TABLE: FURNITURE

PROJECT — TABLE

BULLETIN BOARD — PAPER

CHAPTER 5
COMMON ITEMS/UNCOMMON USES

Music Stands

As a result of their rectangular top, music stands used individually and in groups can be adjusted to represent a number of rectangular three-dimensional objects. When the top of the stand is placed in a horizontal position and paper or cloth has been draped from it, the basic shape is rectangular. Items such as vending machines, phone booths, washing machines, dryers, refrigerators, and U. S. Post Office mailboxes can be easily made in this manner. With the top of the music stand in a horizontal position and the paper covering hung from it, details depicting the desired object can be painted on.

Coat Racks

Many free-standing coat racks can be used as the internal framework for a number of very useful objects and structures. Since these racks are normally about 5 feet in height, they lend themselves to the typical booth-style structure; however, the location of the lower supports on some racks may eliminate them from considerations. If the coat rack you are considering does not provide for safe footing at the base, do not use it. Any small rectangular structure such as a ticket booth, puppet theater, lemonade stand, bridge for a ship, or even a chicken coop, can be made from a coat rack. Illustration 5-12 demonstrates how a coat rack can be used as the internal framework for a lemonade stand. In the case of the lemonade stand, the coat rack is covered with bulletin board paper and the required details painted on.

SUPPORTS FOR SET PIECES AND BACKDROPS

Occasionally a director has a need to obtain supports for mini-scene backdrops and/or set pieces. There are also other instances where the director has neither a permanent means of hanging a backdrop nor a system of frames for supporting scenery. In either case, the director's search should begin with a thorough review of available items and equipment. This section will provide a number of applicable alternatives for the resolution of backdrop or set-piece-related problems.

Stepladders

With the addition of long 2" x 3" or 2" x 4" crosspieces, high stepladders may be used to support sizable backdrops. Use wood clamps to secure the crosspieces firmly to the top step of each ladder. Staple the top of the backdrop to the crosspieces and allow it to hang to the floor.

Chair/Coat Storage Racks

The chair/coat rack depicted in Illustration 5-7 can also be used to support a backdrop or serve as a framework for a set piece. While large enough to serve quite well as a set piece holder, the lower height of this rack restricts its use for students beyond fifth grade. When using this rack, scenery may be taped to the top bar and allowed to drape to the floor. If your performance area is large enough to allow the rack to be turned around during the course of the production, you can suspend a different scene from the other side of this rack.

5-12
COAT RACK: LEMONADE STAND

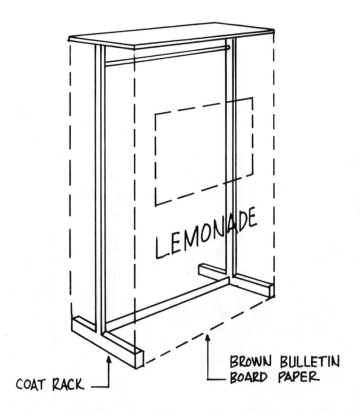

COAT RACK

BROWN BULLETIN
BOARD PAPER

LEMONADE

Privacy Screens
and Portable Room Dividers

Privacy screens and portable room dividers are usually relatively small and therefore lend themselves to presentations conducted in confined areas. Because of their size, it is usually necessary to use two or more screen dividers for any given production. Here again, the backdrop may be taped to the top of the framework and allowed to hang to the floor. When planning mini-scenes (occuring outside of the main performance area), screens and dividers can be a viable means of enhancing the desired illusion.

Free-Standing Chalkboards
and Dry Erase Writing Boards

When used in groups of two or more, these portable writing surfaces provide an excellent framework for the suspension of backdrop materials. If equipped with wheels, each side of the board can be dedicated to a particular backdrop setting. As was the case with the privacy screens and portable room dividers, these pieces of equipment lend themselves to mini-scenes and productions conducted in confined areas.

Music Stands

Music stands may be used to support set pieces or set props (props such as a fence). If a city skyline is to serve as a set piece which will be placed in front of a blue sky backdrop, music stands can be used to support the skyline.

CHAPTER 5
COMMON ITEMS/UNCOMMON USES

Illustration 5-13 provides details for ways the skyline may be attached to a group of music stands. Back-lighting the skyline adds a professional touch to this effective combination of set piece and backdrop.

Volleyball Stanchions

Volleyball stanchions may serve as a very efficient means of hanging a backdrop. Duct tape, bailing wire, or clamps can be used to attach a crosspiece to the top of the volleyball stanchions. The backdrop is then secured to the cross piece and allowed to drape to the floor. In order to assure safety and stability, the crosspiece you select should not be composed of a heavy material. A long bamboo pole is an ideal cross piece. In order to prevent excessive sagging in the middle of the crosspiece, allow 2 to 3 feet of it to extend past the attachment point on each stanchion.

5-13
MUSIC STAND SET PIECE: SKYLINE

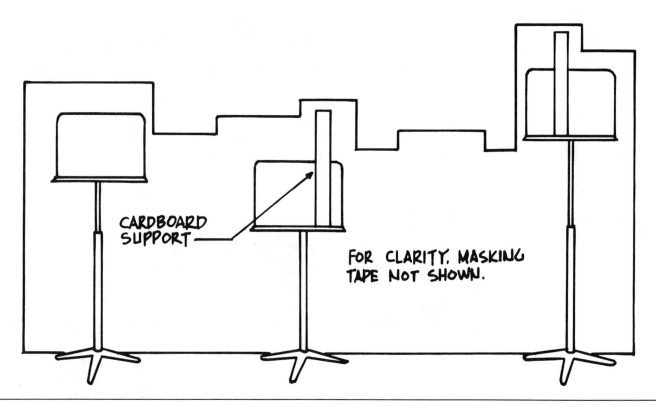

CARDBOARD SUPPORT

FOR CLARITY, MASKING TAPE NOT SHOWN.

Tripod Projection Screens

Two or more tripod projection screens may be used effectively as backdrop supports. The screens should be erected and placed in their normal position. Then the backdrop material may be suspended from the top of the screen and extend to the floor; however, the front leg of the tripod will prevent the backdrop from hanging unencumbered. By cutting a slit in the paper backdrop, the front leg of the tripod will be allowed to pass though. The exposed leg can be covered with backdrop material making its presence less obvious to the audience.

CHAPTER 5
COMMON ITEMS/UNCOMMON USES

NOTES

CHAPTER 6

BASIC LIGHTING AND SPECIAL EFFECTS

Gymnasiums and all-purpose rooms lend themselves to a seemingly endless variety of events and activities. When it comes to theatrical production; however, these areas literally leave us in the dark! If a professional lighting technician were to be given the resources of the typical director and then asked to produce a play in a gym or all-purpose room, he or she would be confronted with obstacles eclipsing those presented by many professional theatrical productions. With this in mind, it is not unusual to find directors who simply eliminate lighting considerations from their production planning schedules. This chapter is intended as a guide for directors who must conduct their performances in areas not originally intended for theatrical presentations. Those who are fortunate enough to have a well-equipped formal stage are congratulated and encouraged to proceed to the section devoted to special effects.

It has become apparent that lighting is one of the most frequently neglected program components in many amateur and children's theatrical productions. The suggestions contained within should encourage directors to confidently confront this demanding challenge.

LIGHTING CONTROL

The obstacles associated with gym and all-purpose room lighting can be summarized into three major areas of concern: 1.) entire lighting banks controlled by one switch; 2.) slow-starting energy-saving fixtures; 3.) uncontrolled (natural or artificial source) light entering the performance area. The main objective of this section will be to first define each problem and then pose some viable alternatives for dealing with them.

The initial reason many directors have abandoned lighting plans can be attributed to the absence of basic room lighting controls. In large rooms, it is not unusual to have lighting fixtures grouped together in multiple banks. In turn, these banks are controlled by a few switches, thereby making it impossible to select the desired lighting schematic. At times, these awkward lighting arrangements seem to conspire against the will of the director. Regardless of careful planning, our inability to turn on and off specific lighting fixtures usually results in either too much or too little light.

A further complication arises when the performance hall is equipped with slow-start energy-saving fixtures. These fixtures prohibit the use of intentional blackouts. Once turned off, they take from 5 to 10 minutes to regain full illumination. If the script contains a nightfall scene followed by a sunrise, there is no better way to orchestrate it than with lighting of this type. Given the improbability of being able to take advantage of this singular attribute, a resolution to the problem remains to be found.

Unwelcomed light from sources outside of the performance hall can totally undermine all of your efforts to develop a meaningful lighting scheme. Unless unwanted light can be controlled, all other efforts to improve lighting will be greatly diminished. In the theater, both darkness and light play an equally significant role.

While there may not be a solution to the lighting impediments mentioned above, steps can be taken to reduce the director's concerns. The following four lighting improvement approaches are worthy of your consideration.

Suggestion 1: Position the Performance

The first step in gaining some control over your situation is to become thoroughly conversant with the illumination pattern imposed by the lighting banks in your performance hall. While it may be impossible to turn individual fixtures on and off, you can at least have some influence over general areas of illumination. Your main objective should be to position your performance area in a location which presents the best alternatives for stage lighting.

If the lighting banks run **perpendicular** to the front of the stage, use of existing lighting fixtures is greatly limited. Lighting banks running **parallel** to the front

of the stage present the greatest number of options. Illustration 6-1 shows two typical examples of ceiling lighting arrangements. Example A depicts a situation in which the director cannot fully illuminate the stage without turning on most, if not all, of the house-lights. Example B allows the director to turn off all lighting banks except #1 providing illumination for the stage while minimizing lighting in the areas occupied by the audience. Assuming one switch controls bank #1, the director has the option of turning it off during certain scenes and augmenting it with supplemental lighting.

When lighting banks run perpendicular to the front of the stage, the director is faced with a significant lighting control problem. If possible, it would be advantageous to position the performance area (assuming the stage is not built-in) in a location parallel to existing banks of lighting. If this cannot be done, explore the possibility of investing in one or more of the supplemental lighting schemes discussed in the next section.

Suggestion 2: Add a Ceiling Bank

In the absence of a lighting bank pattern which can be used for stage illumination, the director must consider other alternatives. For example, in one particular school, performances were conducted in the gym. The lighting banks in this facility were arranged in such an arbitrary manner as to prohibit any organized approach to stage lighting. This situation was resolved with the installation of a separate ceiling bank of floodlight-style fixtures focused on the main performance area. While this solution did entail some cost, it proved to be useful for a number of events and therefore well worth the additional expenditure. The installation of a special bank of lights was well within the range of projects usually undertaken by the P.T.A. or other parent service groups.

Suggestion 3: Use Blackout Material

As previously stated, unless light from sources outside the performance hall can be controlled, all of your efforts related to lighting may be less effective. Here again, the solution rests with the acquisition of funds which will provide for the installation of curtains and or opaque shades. This is another long-term project for consideration by parent and local service groups.

6-1
CEILING LIGHTING BANKS AND STAGE LOCATION

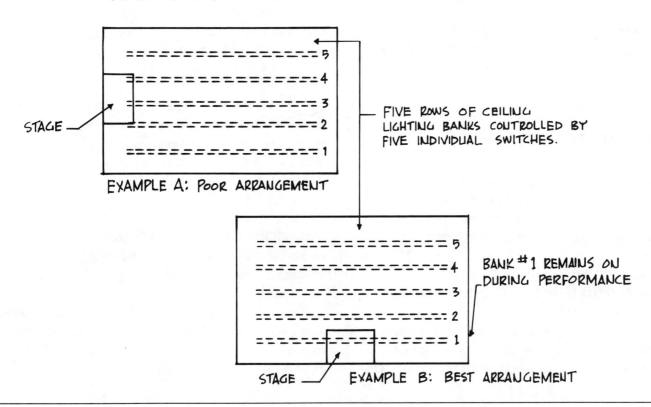

STAGE

FIVE ROWS OF CEILING LIGHTING BANKS CONTROLLED BY FIVE INDIVIDUAL SWITCHES.

EXAMPLE A: POOR ARRANGEMENT

BANK #1 REMAINS ON DURING PERFORMANCE

STAGE — EXAMPLE B: BEST ARRANGEMENT

CHAPTER 6
BASIC LIGHTING AND SPECIAL EFFECTS

In the absence of a long-term solution, blackout paper can be used. Putting up blackout material is usually a time-consuming task; however, it is a worthwhile procedural step.

Suggestion 4: Add Supplemental Lighting
The installation of the additional lighting bank noted in Suggestion 2 is a critical basic component, but it contributes little to the drama and excitement of your production. In order to include these elements in your presentation, it is necessary to provide controllable lighting supplements. In cases where the permanent installation of a separate ceiling bank is not a realistic expectation, supplemental lighting is an absolute requirement. The next section provides a number of alternatives which may prove to be of some assistance in this area.

SUPPLEMENTAL LIGHTING

There are three possible sources for supplemental lighting. Equipment may be: 1.) rented; 2.) borrowed; and/or 3.) derived from standard lighting fixtures. The main focus of this section will be the use of standard lighting fixtures.

Rented and Borrowed Equipment
As you might assume, it is an absolute joy to work with rented professional lighting equipment. Unfortunately, opportunities to rent equipment infrequently present themselves to the director of children's productions. On some occasions it might be possible to borrow equipment from high school and amateur theater groups; however, you may be confronted with a scheduling problem. It is frequently difficult to plan productions to take place during periods when the borrowed equipment is not needed. That is why standard fixtures are preferred allowing productions to be planned according to readily available lighting equipment.

In order to achieve a desired special effect, occasionally it may be necessary to rent equipment. If this is the case, most likely you will be renting one item such as a movable spotlight, strobe light(s), or black light. The cost of renting just the desired unit may not be prohibitive. If it is financially feasible, try incorporating some of these special effects into your productions.

WARNING: Theatrical lighting draws a great deal of electrical current and must be equipped with wiring and circuit breakers designed to handle the load. Licensed personnel must be engaged in the set-up and inspection of this equipment.

Standard Lighting Fixtures
One of the most useful pieces of supplemental lighting equipment is the standard clip-on light. These units can be purchased from a local hardware store and should: 1.) be certified to accept up to a 100-watt bulb; 2.) be equipped with a wide metal reflector; and 3.) have an electrical cord at least 5 feet in length. Do not purchase clip-on lights equipped with fiberglass reflectors.

Two of the major attributes of clip-on lights are minimal weight and ease of mounting. As opposed to professional-style theatrical lighting, sophisticated equipment is not needed to support a bank of clip-on lights. When set up on the sides of the main performance area they can be attached to ladders, volleyball stanchions, music stands, or the lighting support pictured in Illustration 6-2. This is an easily made support and requires little in the way of time or materials. See Illustration 6-3 for construction details. If you plan to set the clip-on lights in front of your performance area, depending on the height of your stage, you may use music stands, student desks, chair backs, or even physical education hurdles to support the lights. These units are versatile and can be arranged around the performance area, but they must be augmented with houselighting. If a fade-out is needed during the course of your production, you may turn off the clip-on lights in groups. This is accomplished by plugging them into multi-receptacle power bars each equipped with a fuse and an on/off switch.

Standard floodlight units may also be used as a means of augmenting the lighting for school productions. These units yield a great deal of light and help fill the void created by the absence of professional lighting equipment. Since floodlight bulbs are also available in a number of useful colors (green, red, blue, and orange), they function like the multi-colored gels available for spotlights. Colored floodlights do not contribute a great deal to the illumination of the stage, but they greatly enhance the vibrancy of the colors you have incorporated into scenery and costumes. Through the teaming of various colors, a number of special effects can be created.

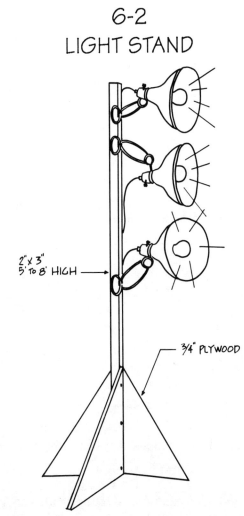

**6-2
LIGHT STAND**

2" x 3"
5' to 8' HIGH

3/4" PLYWOOD

Floodlights may be somewhat difficult to support; however, if you select units equipped with utility-style bases, you will have less difficulty in mounting them. Do not purchase floodlight units with spiked bases. They are designed to be spiked into the ground and therefore provide no means for mounting.

6-3
LIGHT STAND

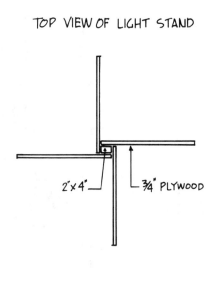

TOP VIEW OF LIGHT STAND

2"x 4"   ¾" PLYWOOD

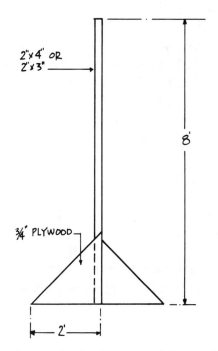

SIDE VIEW LIGHT STAND

2"x 4" OR 2"x 3"

8'

¾" PLYWOOD

2'

When set on the side of the performance area, floodlights may be attached securely to volleyball stanchions. If you plan to use them as footlights, they can easily be mounted on wide and stable boards.

(?) Floodlights cannot be left unattended or in an area where children will have direct access to them. When turned on, they are very hot. All combustible material must be kept far away from floodlights. These units draw a great deal of electricity and must be used with heavy-duty extension cords. Be sure qualified personnel install, inspect and operate your set-up.

Extension cords should be taped down with gaffer's tape. This tape is specially designed for easy removal. It has excellent holding power, yet it generally does not mar or discolor floors. This tape has also been designed to leave a minimal amount of sticky residue on wires and other surfaces. Usually it can be purchased from businesses that rent theatrical equipment, or sound and audio equipment. (Duct tape is sometimes substituted, but can become sticky, may mar surfaces and is not easy to remove.) Unfortunately, gaffer's tape is typically not available in hardware stores.

BASIC SPECIAL EFFECTS

Compared to the professional theater, the special lighting effects described here are somewhat primitive, yet they are an effective means of contributing to the general illusion created by the play. Everything suggested in this section can be accomplished easily and does not require undertaking an extensive search for equipment or materials.

Overhead Projector Techniques

1. A roving spotlight (horizontal movement only) may be simulated with the aid of an overhead projector and a projector cart equipped with casters. Place the cart in the audience. Using a number of sheets of black construction paper, cut out circles ranging in size from 1 to 4 inches in diameter. Place one sheet at a time on the surface of the overhead projector and experiment with the size of the hole and the focus. Identify the size hole which meets your needs. When it is necessary to move the spotlight, keep the projector in position, but rotate the front wheels of the cart from side-to-side in order to obtain the desired movement. The houselights must be turned off. (Also see later in this chapter: "Slide Projector").

2. If a relatively short mini-scene is required, consider using an overhead projector to simulate the desired background. Using colored markers, draw the required scene on a blank overhead acetate sheet. Project the scene onto a light, neutral background. The performers will cast a shadow onto the background material;

however, in some scenes, this effect actually may be desirable.

3. Background movement of machines, crowds, animals, clouds, etc. can be created with silhouettes cut from black construction paper. These images may be placed on the surface of the overhead projector and moved about to simulate the desired motion. This technique is especially useful for scenes dealing with very large or massive objects in motion. The houselights must be turned off.

4. A scene depicting a large fire can be created with three acetate projection sheets which have been colored with orange, yellow, and red markers. Each of the colored sheets should have flames of equivalent sizes drawn on them. Place the sheets over each other and project them onto a light background. Using the three differently colored flames, move them to simulate the movement of flames in a raging fire. In order to simulate smoke, a fourth sheet may have black puffs drawn on it.

Flashlights

Scenes from outer space or a trip back in time can be simulated by completely darkening your performance hall. All of the children in the cast and chorus should have flashlights equipped in the following manner. Cover the lenses with dark paper permitting only a small circle of light (about the size of a quarter) to shine through. Play appropriate music and direct the children to flash their lights all around the room.

CHAPTER 6
BASIC LIGHTING AND SPECIAL EFFECTS

Flash Camera
Multiple camera flashes (more than one camera is needed) can be used to simulate lightning, distant explosions, cannon fire, a rocket launch, or any other flash-related occurrence. Here again, a completely darkened performance hall is required. The camera flashes should be aimed at the backdrop and not the audience. This technique is most effective when the children operating the cameras cannot be seen.

Back-Lighting Ground Rows
Back-lighting ground rows (low flats placed in front of the backdrop such as a skyline) adds a sense of depth to the scene. Back-lighting is a low-tech approach which gives a high-tech appearance. This technique is especially effective with nighttime or sunset-style scenes.

Christmas Lights
Mini-bulb, all-white Christmas lights can be employed to serve a number of useful purposes. Obtain the type equipped with a control for brightness and blinking rate. Listed below are three possible applications.

1. A Broadway-style set can be given a professional appearance if the blinking lights are incorporated into the theater marquees.

2. A scene depicting a night sky can be greatly enhanced with blinking white lights. This approach can be applied to stars in a desert sky or city lights associated with a silhouette of a distant city skyline. Create an all-black backdrop (bulletin board paper) and make small holes for the lights. Tape the connecting wires to the back of the backdrop. Reinforce the backdrop with duct tape. Because of its weight, this type of backdrop should not exceed 10 feet in height. If not properly reinforced with duct tape, the backdrop will tear when you attempt to hang it.

3. Outer space themes offer a number of excellent opportunities to incorporate blinking white lights into background sets and various forms of spacecraft. Large electrical panels come to life when blinking lights are integrated into the controls.

Slide Projectors
Slide projectors can be adapted to serve as substitute spotlights. Using a slide that can be discarded, or the blank slide which usually accompanies a newly-developed set of slides, blacken both sides of the slide with magic marker. Use a hole-punch to make a hole in the center of the slide. Once placed in a slide projector, the blackened slide will project a circular spot of light.

1. Using this technique, various shapes can be cut out of the blackened slide. Heart-, oval-, star-, and square-shaped, etc. light patterns can be projected.

2. If you would like a circular shape (or other) to increase or decrease in size, create a set of blackened slides with incrementally larger (or smaller) cutouts. By projecting the slides in order of size (of the cutout), it will appear that the circle of light is changing size incrementally.

CHAPTER 7

PROPS AND SET PIECES

Much of what we do in theater is an illusion. This illusion, mirage, or fantasy is conveyed through images created with a host of elements including dialogue, music, action, costumes, scenery, and lighting. Well-designed props can augment and unify a number of the diverse components that contribute to the quality of your production. The main objective of this chapter is to provide you with the techniques needed to build credible, yet easily constructed, props and set pieces.

BASIC PROP PATTERNS

One of the most time-consuming aspects of prop construction is the need to search for patterns or illustrations of required items. In order to facilitate your efforts, patterns depicting frequently used props have been provided. In order to expedite the duplication process, illustration details have been kept to a minimum.

Two methods of duplication are suggested. If you will be constructing a large item such as the sleigh, trace it onto an acetate sheet which can then be placed on an overhead projector. Project the image onto the material that will serve as the prop. Trace the image and cut it to the desired shape. An opaque projector can be used to project smaller props such as the barrel or fire hydrant directly from this book (tracing step is skipped) onto the intended prop

material. Actually, either method will produce the desired results; however, the overhead projector produces a better image of larger objects.

An excellent source of additional prop ideas can be found within the pages of illustrated children's books. The illustrations in these books are usually simplified versions of the real object thereby facilitating your efforts to replicate the shape and style of the desired object.

The following is a list of the prop patterns included at the end of this chapter. Also additional patterns can be found in Chapter 8 devoted to inflatable props.

ILLUSTRATED PROP PATTERNS

GROUND ROWS: IDEAS AND APPLICATIONS

With the inclusion of a ground row, many outdoor scenes can be transformed into realistic and colorful settings. Whether the ground row appears in the form of a distant skyline or a nearby fence, this useful device is sure to enliven your production.

Fences

Only a minimal amount of effort is needed to create a split-rail or picket fence. Both of these items can contribute a great deal to a scene involving characters in a rural or suburban setting. A fence not only adds depth to the scene, it provides numerous staging options. Characters can walk around, lean on, or talk over a fence. This simple prop incorporates another dimension into your staging options.

(?) **When constructing the split-rail or picket fence, take special care to see that the sharp points of the fasteners do not protrude through to the other side.**

Making a Split-Rail Fence

To build a split-rail fence, consult the construction details provided in Illustration 7-21. Build the end supports on the floor, taking care to observe the overlapped joints designated in the illustration. In order for the fence to be free-standing, it will be necessary to construct two or more sections. Sections should not exceed 8 feet in length.

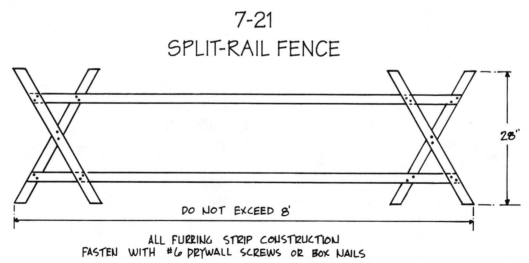

7-21
SPLIT-RAIL FENCE

28"

DO NOT EXCEED 8'

ALL FURRING STRIP CONSTRUCTION
FASTEN WITH #6 DRYWALL SCREWS OR BOX NAILS

Fence segments can be attached by overlapping and wiring together (cover wire ends with tape) the crossed portion of the end supports. The angle between the segments should not exceed 120°.

Making a Picket Fence

Unlike the split-rail fence, the picket fence consists of a combination of furring strips and paper (or oak tag) rungs. Furring strips are used only where structural support is required. This approach saves time and materials. See Illustration 7-22 for construction details. Here again, two or more fence sections are needed if the fence is to be free-standing. Wire the sections together making sure that the angle between the segments does not exceed 120°.

NATURAL BORDERS

Ice Skating Scenes

With the inclusion of an 8- to 10-inch high ground row, you can realistically simulate an ice skating scene. In this case, the ground row consists of a white puffy border placed 4 feet (depending on sight lines and configuration of performance area) in from the front of your performance area. The border can be made easily from the white foam panels discussed in the section on "Prop Construction Materials." The white border represents the snow usually shoveled to the sides of ice skating ponds. It also serves as a means of masking the surface of the stage from the view of the audience. Children on roller blades and

7-22
PICKET FENCE

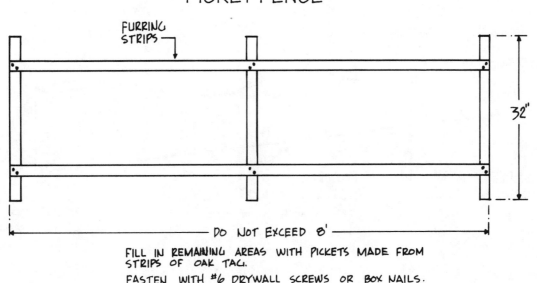

FURRING STRIPS

32"

DO NOT EXCEED 8'

FILL IN REMAINING AREAS WITH PICKETS MADE FROM STRIPS OF OAK TAG.
FASTEN WITH #6 DRYWALL SCREWS OR BOX NAILS.

dressed in winter clothing can glide gently and slowly back and forth simulating an outdoor skating scene. See Illustration 7-23 for details regarding the construction of the foam panel border.

(?) **This ice skating scene is intended for performance areas that are on the same level as the audience. Stages with orchestra pits should not, under any circumstances, be used to conduct this scene. The children selected to participate in this scene must be skilled roller blade skaters. It is essential that they know how to turn and come to a safe stop.**

Waves and Water

As primitive as it may seem, the old vaudevillian method for depicting waves still gets a chuckle and applause from parents. To depict people in the water or in a boat, use wave groups that are $1^{1/2}$ to 2 feet high. In order to make this type of ground row, simply cut waves out of long lengths of corrugated cardboard (paint green/blue with white highlights) and staple them to the edge of a long 2" x 3". You can add motion to the waves by creating a slightly higher second row which will appear behind the shorter row. Both rows can be moved back and forth in a gentle reciprocal motion.

7-23
SNOW BORDER: ICE SKATING SCENE

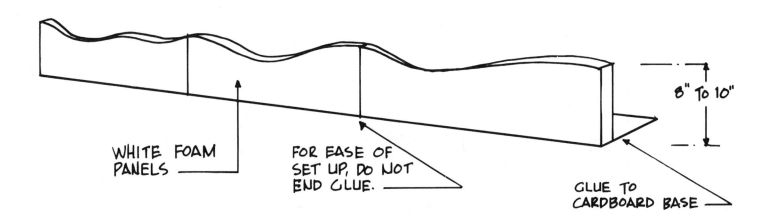

WHITE FOAM PANELS

FOR EASE OF SET UP, DO NOT END GLUE.

8" TO 10"

GLUE TO CARDBOARD BASE

Bush Borders and Hedges

Hedges present the same staging advantages as fences. They can be made by stapling green bulletin board paper to the fence frame shown in Illustration 7-22. Cut the top portion of the bulletin board paper in a manner simulating the bush or hedge silhouette. Paint on details including brown branches and dark-green highlights.

FLAT SET PIECES

Two-Dimensional Objects/ Three-Dimensional Perspective

A basic set design challenge stems from the need to convey the illusion of distance and depth within a small area. Given the space required to accommodate real three-dimensional objects, the director must turn to flat or relatively flat shapes to address this requirement. Equipped with techniques used by pictorial artists, the director can add a sense of depth to a number of settings.

Along with a host of other techniques, the pictorial artist uses various planes to create the illusion of depth. The director can use different flats to invoke a sense of perspective by using three different planes (background, middleground, and foreground). Illustration 7-24 demonstrates how this can be accomplished.

You will note that the three planes consist of the following objects: 1.) the backdrop depicting sky and mountains; 2.) free-standing tree clusters; and 3.) ground row bushes.

The illusion of depth can also be enhanced with the careful application of tonal values and painted details. When pictorial artists lay out the various planes contained in their paintings, progressively lighter tonal values are used as they move from the foreground to the background. Details are handled with the same guideline in mind. A piece in the foreground will be highly detailed, while a background object should have only a vague representation of detail.

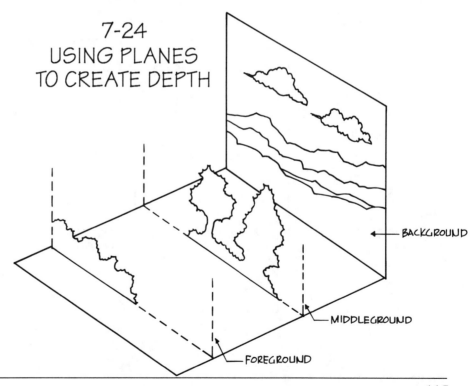

7-24
USING PLANES
TO CREATE DEPTH

BACKGROUND

MIDDLEGROUND

FOREGROUND

CHAPTER 7
PROPS AND SET PIECES

TWO USEFUL SET PIECES

This section includes construction details for two objects that can positively contribute to many different settings. The first object, a free-standing tree, offers a wide span of applications ranging from a city street to an uninhabited forest. The second object, a curtained stage front, is not seen frequently, but is one which may be considered for a number of special situations.

Free-Standing Tree

Chapter 5 offers several suggestions regarding the creation of free-standing trees; however, all of these trees are single-use items which are discarded at the conclusion of the production. If you have even minimal storage space, consider making one or more of these trees. Each tree consists of a two-part base (trunk and support) plus three foliage supports. See Illustrations 7-25 and 7-26. The foliage should be paper that can be changed to represent a wide variety of trees. The paper portion is stapled onto the foliage supports (furring strips) and may be discarded after each production. Once disassembled for storage purposes, this free-standing tree lies flat and occupies very little space. Considering the number of occasions when you will use these trees, it makes good sense to build one or more of them. Your initial expenditure is an investment that will eventually result in the saving of precious time and money.

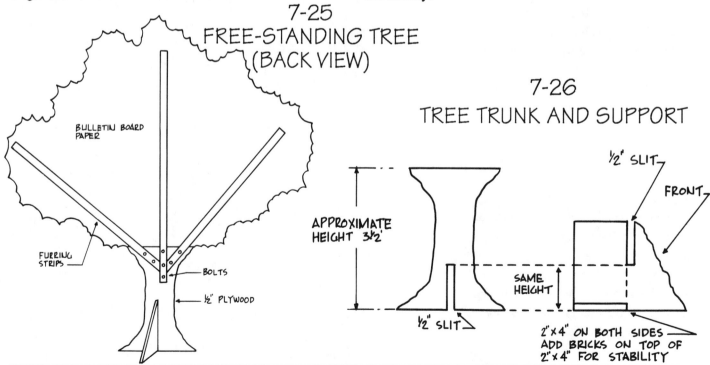

7-25
FREE-STANDING TREE
(BACK VIEW)

BULLETIN BOARD PAPER

FURRING STRIPS

BOLTS

½" PLYWOOD

7-26
TREE TRUNK AND SUPPORT

APPROXIMATE HEIGHT 3½'

½" SLIT

½" SLIT

FRONT

SAME HEIGHT

2"x4" ON BOTH SIDES
ADD BRICKS ON TOP OF
2"x4" FOR STABILITY

Curtained Stage Front

Even if you have a formal stage, this useful set piece may prove to be a handy addition to your repertoire of props. Directors who do not have a curtained stage will find many applications for this piece. Some of the uses include: 1.) staging a play within a play; 2.) talent shows; 3.) vaudeville acts; and 4.) circus-style productions. Illustration 7-27 depicts the stage front as it might appear in a vaudeville-style production.

Because of the cost of lumber and problems related to storage, the stage front was not designed to be a reusable prop; however, if carefully disassembled, the parts can be saved and used again. This set piece was designed as a false stage front, (the curtains are really paper painted to appear as if they were pleated and tied back); the curtain is therefore always in the opened position. A backdrop covering the backstage area is needed to complete the illusion. The wood used to make the stage front is not strong enough to support heavy objects or a real cloth

7-27
STAGE CURTAIN AND SET PIECE

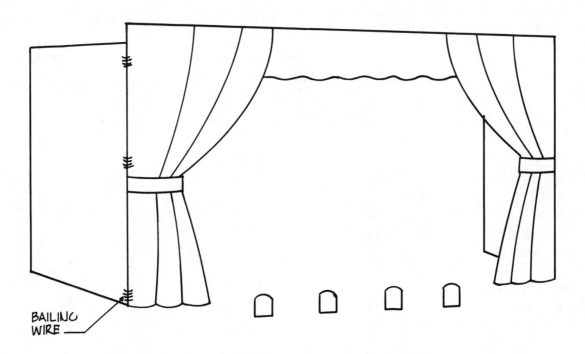

BAILING
WIRE

curtain. Construction details appear in Illustration 7-28. This set piece requires a side corner brace on each end. Each brace should be wired to the main section at three locations (see Illustration 7-27). These braces are constructed the same as the "Tall Side Support Brace" shown in Illustration 3-15.

PROP CONSTRUCTION MATERIALS

This section is devoted to a brief discussion of easily obtained materials that may be used for prop construction. Whether you intend to build the props suggested within, or make props of your own design, the following materials review should assist you with making decisions regarding which materials will work best.

Corrugated Cardboard Panels

Corrugated cardboard panels are useful for a number of applications. These panels can be supported without difficulty or complication. The brown paper surface will accept without priming the inexpensive water based paints frequently found in schools. Since they can be easily bent, cut, and taped into

a wide variety of shapes, corrugated panels can be used to simulate a large number of items. The light weight of these panels makes it possible for children to handle and position props easily. In some areas they can be purchased from a variety of vendors, while in other areas these panels are quite difficult to locate. If you can obtain cardboard panels, consider incorporating them into your plans for prop construction.

Furring Strips

The numerous attributes of furring strips have been noted throughout this book. They are inexpensive, relatively

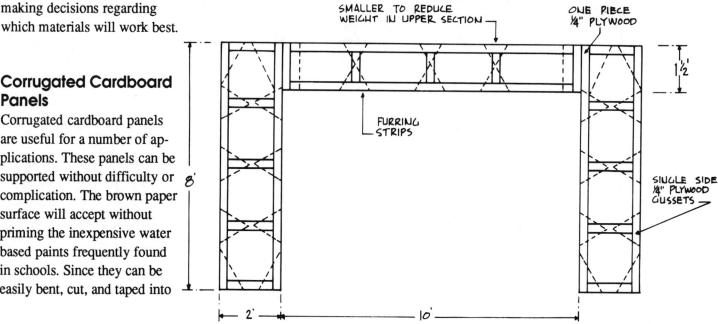

7-28

CONSTRUCTION DETAILS: STAGE AND CURTAIN

SMALLER TO REDUCE WEIGHT IN UPPER SECTION

ONE PIECE ¼" PLYWOOD

FURRING STRIPS

SINGLE SIDE ¼" PLYWOOD GUSSETS

light weight, readily available, and extremely versatile. Furring strips are usually available in two or three different thicknesses with lengths ranging from 7 to 12 feet. The one objectionable characteristic of furring strips is that they are usually made from poor-quality wood. This makes it necessary for you to purchase approximately 12 percent more wood then you actually need. Furring strips that are bent or filled with knots should not be used for applications requiring lengths beyond 3 feet.

Cardboard Boxes

Cardboard boxes usually can be obtained free of charge. Because they come in a wide variety of shapes and sizes, careful advance planning will assure you of having all you need. For example, groups of similarly shaped boxes can be used to make a fireplace, simulated stone wall, or serve as props for a circus act. Large boxes (especially appliance boxes) can be cut into a number of useful shapes. Remember, most boxes can be folded flat and stored easily for use in future productions. It might be a good idea to keep a small stash on hand.

Foam Panels

Foam insulation panels can be purchased from almost any lumberyard. Though somewhat expensive, the cost is within the range of most production budgets. The two panel sizes that are readily available are: 3/4" x 13⅝" x 48" and 1" x 2' x 8'. As a result of their light weight and the ease with which they can be cut, these panels have a broad range of applications. Foam panels can be easily glued into a number of shapes. Use relatively inexpensive vinyl adhesive caulk to bond panels. This adhesive requires 24 hours to cure; however, it forms a glue line which is stronger than the foam. Use enough adhesive to permit a bead of glue to seep out of each side of the glue line. Foam panels are an excellent choice for free-standing props. Simply glue a triangular foam support to the back of the prop. The very light weight of these props permits them to be handled by small children.

Builder's Tubes

Builder's tubes are firm cardboard cylinders used as forms for cylindrical cement (construction) footings. They come in a variety of diameters ranging in size from approximately 8 inches to 24 inches and are available in a number of different lengths. Large tubes are somewhat heavy and therefore not practical for all applications. The smaller sizes are more useful in children's productions. These tubes can be cut to the desired size and may be used in settings requiring cylindrical shapes. Compared to the other materials suggested here, builder's tubes are among the most expensive to purchase.

Lauan Plywood

When props must have a fair degree of structural strength, consider using 1/4-inch lauan plywood. It is more costly than the other panel materials noted above; however, it is relatively inexpensive when compared to other structurally sound sheet materials. Lauan is easy to work with and is not as heavy as most wooden paneling. If you have sufficient room for prop storage, those frequently used can be made out of lauan. This approach will ultimately result in saving time and money.

CHAPTER 7
PROPS AND SET PIECES

7-1
FIRE HYDRANT

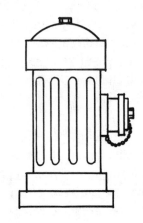

7-2
RAIN BARREL

7-3
DICKENS ERA LAMPPOST

7-4
STEAMER TRUNK

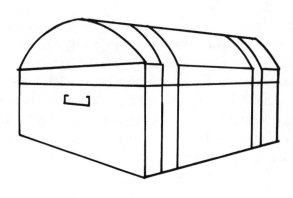

7-5
PALM TREE

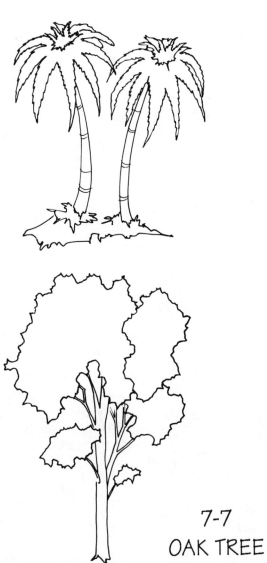

7-6
WEEPING WILLOW TREE

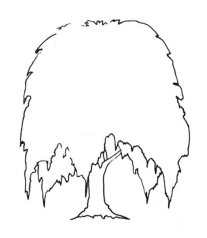

7-7
OAK TREE

7-8
EVERGREEN TREE

CHAPTER 7
PROPS AND SET PIECES

7-9
DOCK PILINGS

7-10
SLEIGH

7-11
REINDEER

7-12
COW

7-13
HORSE

7-14
ELEPHANT

7-15
LION

7-16
APE

7-17
TYRANNOSAURUS REX

7-18
COVERED WAGON

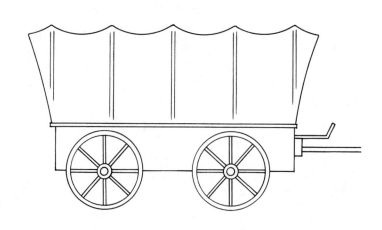

7-19
STAGE COACH

7-20
SCHOOL BUS

CHAPTER 8

INFLATABLE SETS AND PROPS

If you are looking for a unique special effect that is a total departure from approaches usually taken in amateur and children's theater, consider the construction of inflatable set pieces and props. If sufficient time is set aside for the construction process, inflatables can contribute to the enthusiasm of your performers as well as add a new dimension to your productions. The ease with which inflatables can be stored and saved for future productions makes them an especially attractive alternative.

Here are some applications for inflatables in your productions.

1. If a monster or giant plant makes its entrance by coming to life or growing right before the eyes of the audience, an inflatable prop can be employed to convey this illusion. In order to perform this bit of theatrical magic, a vacuum cleaner is used to inflate the prop during the course of the production.

2. In Chapter 1, mention was made of "theater-in-the-half-round." If you will be conducting performances with this type of configuration, inflatable sets and props can be a real plus. While the inflatable design suggested here does not yield a true three-dimensional object, it provides a sufficient amount of shape to convey the desired effect.

3. Scenes taking place in a Lilliputian-style world can benefit from large inflatable props. If the setting calls for a large high-top shoe or a huge mushroom, an inflatable prop may meet your needs.

4. An inflatable ground row may be used effectively in a number of situations – hedges can grow on the spot, mountains can suddenly come into view, or stone walls can appear from nowhere. A ground row designed to simulate waves could be used when portraying an actor going deeper and deeper into the surf. As the actor goes into the surf (ground row of waves), the ground row is inflated giving the illusion that the performer is going down in the water.

PRELIMINARY CONSIDERATIONS

The successful construction of an inflatable prop can be an enjoyable and rewarding experience; however, before planning to incorporate this technique into your next production, some thought must be given to the following requirements.

CHAPTER 8
INFLATABLE SETS AND PROPS

CONSTRUCTION REQUIREMENTS

If the set or prop you are planning to make needs to be inflated for only a short time during the production (example: ground row waves) and then allowed to deflate, the challenge of making this type of prop is not beyond the skill of the average person. If you plan to make a prop that is to remain inflated during your **entire** production, a higher level of craftsmanship is required. Since reasonably priced plastic film has flaws which ultimately result in air leakage, greater care must be exercised in the construction of an inflatable that is to retain its intended shape for 30 minutes or more.

Based upon the attitude and skill level of the volunteers making your inflatable, this process can be an enjoyable challenge. Since no two situations are alike, it is not possible to provide a "no-fail recipe" for success. The individuals involved in the process must be able to follow the steps provided within, while being prepared to make adjustments to comply with the specific needs of your situation. *Inflatables have what I refer to as a high "fiddle factor." In order to achieve the desired results, you frequently have to "fiddle" around a bit before you get it right.* Because of unpredictable variables, work on your inflatable must be started weeks before your production is to take place. You must give yourself sufficient time to either correct an error or make a substitute prop or set.

If you can recruit a group of skilled and patient volunteers, consider including an inflatable in a future production. Individuals who engage in craft-style hobbies are usually better equipped to deal with the challenges and variables associated with the construction of inflatables.

APPLICATION REQUIREMENTS

The inflatables discussed within consist of two sheets of plastic film which form what would be equivalent to an inflated pillow. These inflatables have distinct characteristics that determine how and where they can be employed. Since they cannot be pressurized to the point where they totally support themselves, any inflatable exceeding 3 feet in height must be held up by some external means.

If you plan to design your own inflatable, it will be necessary to slightly exaggerate the width of each object. Once inflated, a portion of the plastic film is drawn forward reducing the apparent width of the object. Assuming you want to make a giant mushroom with a stem approximately $1^{1/2}$-feet wide, it is best to exceed this width on your pattern by 4 to 5 inches.

One of the main features of the inflatable is that it can be folded and stored easily for future use. If you have painted or coated your inflatable, it is advisable to place wax paper between each fold. Unpainted inflatables may simply be rolled up and placed in storage.

Your first inflatable should not be too large. Since a number of construction techniques must be mastered in order to experience success, it is suggested that your first inflatable should be no larger than a 6' x 10' object.

(?) **As with all flammable materials, do not place an inflatable near an open flame.**

LIST OF REQUIRED TOOLS AND MATERIALS

Tools

1. An iron that can be used for craft-related projects (there is a chance some melted plastic may get on the iron).
2. Scissors.
3. Vacuum cleaner with the capability to be used in the exhaust mode.
4. An overhead projector or an opaque projector if you will be making a pattern.

Materials

1. Black plastic film that is 4 millimeters thick. Obtain the same quality sheeting as the material used for vapor barriers in home construction. Do not use sheeting thinner than 4 millimeters.
2. Masking tape.
3. White liquid shoe polish with sponge applicator (used to mark pattern on black plastic).
4. Sheets of construction paper to be used in the seam sealing process (the amount depends on the size of your inflatable).
5. Several sheets of newspaper.
6. Sheets of white bulletin board paper which will be taped together to form the pattern upon which the object will be drawn.
7. Duct tape.

(?) **Since several types of plastic sheeting are sold in different parts of the country, it is not possible to recommend a specific type. In order to assure safety, use the following combustibility test to be sure the plastic you are using will not ignite as a result of the application of a hot iron. Conduct this test outdoors in an area away from combustible materials.**

1. Place a 1/2-inch square sample of the plastic you will be using between two pieces of construction paper.
2. Adjust your iron to the hottest setting and place it on top of the construction paper (containing the plastic) for approximately 10 seconds.
3. The plastic should melt, but not ignite.
4. If the plastic ignites, do not use it for your inflatable.

PATTERN MAKING

Contained within this chapter are three common patterns used to make inflatables. They include a dinosaur, giant mushroom, and a high-top boot (Illustrations 8-1, 8-2, and 8-3). Children's books, magazines, and children's artwork are excellent sources for possible patterns. Objects consisting of many thin and intricate details should not be considered for use as inflatables. Remember to exaggerate the width of the thinner sections of your pattern.

1. Use a clear piece of overhead projector acetate to trace the desired object.
2. Tape sheets of white bulletin board paper together and attach them to the wall.
3. Using an overhead projector, project your object onto the bulletin board paper and trace the outline.
4. Remove the paper from the wall and cut out the pattern.

CONSTRUCTION STEPS

(?) **Children should not participate in the construction process. Do not allow molten plastic to come in contact with your skin. It may cause severe burns.**

Seam Making

Prior to beginning the construction steps, first learn the technique required to make an air-tight heat-sealed seam. Your inflatable will not retain air unless these steps are fully mastered. Work on a surface that will not be damaged by the hot iron. Do not work on a wood floor or an unprotected tile floor. The best surface to work on is a cement floor. Using pieces of scrap plastic, practice the following:

1. Fold a piece of construction paper in half and place it under two pieces of plastic.

2. Fold a sheet of newspaper in half to form a piece approximately 4 inches wide and 12 inches long. Place the newspaper on the seam that is to be heat-sealed.
3. Set your iron at a midpoint between low and permanent press. You may have to experiment with this setting to determine an efficient working temperature. If the iron is too hot, it will damage the plastic sheeting.
4. Place the iron on top of the newspaper approximately $1^{1/2}$ inches from the edge of the plastic sheeting. Using light pressure, move the hot iron slowly along the newspaper in one direction.
5. Be sure the iron does not come in contact with the plastic. If the iron comes in contact with the plastic, it will make a hole.
6. Wait until the plastic begins to cool. Start to remove the newspaper from the top and the construction paper from the bottom. If the plastic is stringy and pulls away from itself, you have removed the paper too soon or the heat setting on the iron should be lowered. As the plastic cools, some of the paper will adhere to the plastic indicating you have correctly completed the seam.
7. A correct seam is approximately 1 inch to $1^{1/2}$ inches wide. A good seam is flat and relatively free of ripples.
8. As you work along the seam, periodically check its quality. When the plastic cools, place your hand inside the two pieces of plastic and check the adhesion between the two sheets of plastic. Be sure that the seam is at least 1 inch wide.

CONSTRUCTION STEPS FOR AN INFLATABLE

Select a floor surface that will not be damaged by a hot iron. A smooth cement floor is the best surface. Do not use a wooden floor. Walking on the plastic sheeting can cause pinhole punctures. Be sure to avoid this. Work in a well-ventilated area.

Step 1
Lay two plastic sheets (one on top of the other) on a floor clear of grit or other particles that could puncture the sheeting.

Step 2
Use masking tape to tape the plastic sheets to the floor, then tape the pattern on top of the plastic. Using white liquid shoe polish (with a sponge applicator), trace the pattern onto the plastic. Remove the pattern when the tracing is complete.

Step 3
Cut out the inflatable along the shoe polish lines. Cut both sheets at once making sure the top piece with the pattern outline does not shift. In order to prevent shifting, tape the pieces together approximately every 3 feet along the cut line.

Step 4
When the pattern has been completely cut out, tape the pieces to the floor at intervals of approximately every 3 feet.

Step 5
Working in one direction along the seam line, follow the procedures previously noted for making a heat-sealed seam.

Step 6
During this entire process, do not allow the iron to come in contact with the plastic. If this occurs, mark the area with white shoe polish. This will warn you of an area that may have a leak.

Step 7
Along the bottom of the inflatable, allow a 4-inch segment of the seam to remain unsealed. This is the place where the inflatable will be filled with air.

Step 8
If your inflatable will be taller than 3 feet, use duct tape to put one or more support tabs on the top of the object. Use a double thickness of tape and puncture the tape on top to accommodate a cord from which it can be hung.

Step 9
Prior to inflation, be sure to carefully read and observe the directions appearing on the next page. If it will be necessary for your inflatable to retain its shape during the entire production, you will have to check for leaks. In the event the inflatable does not retain air for the required period of time, see Steps 10 and 11.

Step 10
Fill your inflatable with air. Using a bright light source, check along the seam. Look for areas where the iron may have burned through. If you find a leak, seal it with duct tape.

Step 11

If you have not found a leak and your inflatable continues to loose air, it will be necessary to paint it with a liquid plastic coating. This type of coating comes in the form of a paint or a clear varnish. Inexpensive plastic sheeting sometimes has numerous pinholes. If these holes are not too pervasive, the plastic coating should solve your problem.

INFLATION DIRECTIONS

Because of the poor quality of reasonably priced plastic sheeting, most inflatables cannot retain their shape for more than 1 or 2 hours. Fortunately, few performances in children's theater go beyond this time frame. As previously discussed, there are two possible applications for inflatables. One involves objects inflated for a short duration during the performance (such as the waves discussed on page 125), and the other application involves objects inflated before the performance which remain inflated for the duration of the production. Both of these approaches are discussed below.

INFLATION PRIOR TO THE PERFORMANCE

1. Obtain a vacuum cleaner that can be put in exhaust mode. Be sure it is clean and does not need to be emptied.

2. Tear off a 6-inch piece of duct tape. Place the tape on one side of the inflatable in the area of the 4-inch slit.

3. Using the vacuum in exhaust mode, turn it on and place the nozzle of the hose near the 4-inch slit. Place it close enough to the slit to inflate the object, but do not insert the hose. Too much air will cause a seam to burst.

4. Continue to inflate the object until it assumes its intended shape, but not to the point where the object is unduly stressed. If you do burst a seam, repair the area with duct tape.

5. Once the desired level of inflation is reached, continue to aim the hose in the direction of the 4-inch slit while someone else seals it with the unattached side of the 6-inch strip of duct tape.

6. Avoid unnecessary handling after the object has been inflated.

7. In order for objects higher than 3 feet to stand up and retain the air, they must be supported by some external means. See Construction Step 8.

INFLATION DURING THE PRODUCTION

This approach is used when a monster or giant plant is to appear rising during the production. Given the numerous settings, it is not possible to provide a definitive step-by-step approach. This is a perfect example of the "fiddle factor" mentioned at the beginning of this chapter. In order to get this right for your setting, it will be necessary to fiddle around with it. The following suggestions are offered as general guides.

1. Use duct tape to secure the bottom of your inflatable to the floor.

2. If the object is tall, use monofilament fishing line for the top support.

3. Locate the vacuum cleaner in another room or a hall. Use a length of garden hose to connect the inflatable to the vacuum. The distance from the vacuum to the inflatable is critical and should be checked well before the scheduled performance. If the distance is too great you will have problems inflating the object.

4. Tape the other end of the garden hose to the 4-inch inflation slit in the bottom of the object.

5. Assuming the vacuum is to remain on during the entire time the object is inflated, cut a slit in the top of the object. The slit will allow air to fill and then escape the object. In the absence of this slit, the inflatable will burst a seam. The size of the slit will have to be adjusted to meet the air pressure needs of your inflatable.

6. You can allow your object to deflate slowly by simply turning off the vacuum, or you can change the vacuum hose to the intake port on the vacuum and draw the air out rapidly. The needs of your production will determine the procedure that should be used.

NOTES

CHAPTER 8
INFLATABLE SETS AND PROPS

8-1
INFLATABLE DINOSAUR

8-2
INFLATABLE MUSHROOM

8-3
INFLATABLE BOOT

CHAPTER 9

GETTING THE JOB DONE

This chapter contains the organizational tools that you will need to "Get the job done!" It includes a strategy for volunteer recruitment as well as a blueprint for guiding the efforts of your volunteers. **Use this book to determine WHAT can be done; then use it to show volunteers HOW to make it happen.**

Along with a variety of artistic gifts, competent directors must also possess the ability to encourage others to become active participants in their theatrical productions. Individuals who direct amateur and children's theater are faced with an extensive array of tasks and responsibilities. The difficulty of addressing these tasks is often compounded by the shortage of funds and resources. The success of a production should not be the sole responsibility of one individual, but rather the joint effort of a group of motivated and enthusiastic collaborators.

With the aid of the following organizational tools, directors will have the means to engage and guide a capable contingent of willing and able volunteers. These tools will facilitate your efforts to:

1. Use this book as a construction guide for volunteers.

2. Identify sources of volunteer assistance.
   a.) Develop an approach that encourages involvement.
   b.) Devise a plan to maximize volunteer time and talent.

3. Establish a tradition of long-term volunteer commitment.

USING THIS BOOK TO GUIDE VOLUNTEERS

In order to assist you with directing the efforts of your volunteers, the publisher (Shawnee Press, Inc.) hereby grants the original purchaser limited permission to duplicate building patterns, instructions, and construction steps. Use the suggestions listed below as a guide.

1. Review this book and select the desired props and/or sets.

2. Determine the skills your volunteers must possess in order to complete the projects.

3. Recruit volunteers with the needed skills.

4. Duplicate the required instructions, patterns, and construction details contained within this book.

5. Divide the job into a set of tasks and delegate them to your volunteers.

CHAPTER 9
GETTING THE JOB DONE

Example: The castle set described in Chapter 3 (under the section entitled "Unique Shapes Made From Furring Strip Flats") provides a good example of how this book can be used to guide volunteers. Assuming you want to distribute the task of building this set among a group of volunteers, you could proceed as follows:

For Group 1
Duplicate the materials list for the castle and assign the task of obtaining the materials to a group of volunteers.

For Group 2
Provide copies of the plans for the castle side corners (Illustration 3-15) and the drawing of the furring strip construction details (Illustration 3-16). Ask this group to build just the side corners.

For Group 3
Make copies of Illustrations 3-14 and 3-16. These drawings will guide volunteers in the construction of the center section of the castle set. This group can also be asked to assemble the entire castle set support structure. A copy of Illustration 3-8 (describes the bailing wire bindings) should be provided.

For Group 4
This group can be composed of children under the direction of an adult. The children can attach and paint the bulletin board paper covering to the castle. Provide a copy of Illustration 3-13 to guide their efforts.

SOURCES OF VOLUNTEER ASSISTANCE

During the 26 years I have worked with children, volunteer assistance has played a significant role in the successful outcome of a number of special events and productions. Even in today's world of dual-profession and single-parent families, there appears to be an abundance of willing and able volunteers. While most of the assistance I have received has come from parents, there have been occasions when help came from a number of diverse sources.

This section includes various sources of volunteers along with ways to encourage participation while maximizing volunteer productivity.

Parents
Parents are the primary source of volunteer assistance. Given the busy schedules of most families, it is not sufficient to simply send out a parent letter requesting help. A well-planned parent recruitment program begins with a letter which indicates: 1.) why, where and when help is needed; 2.) the amount of time required; 3.) the tasks that will be undertaken; and 4.) if any special tools should be brought from home. Along with your letter, it is helpful to make some personal appeals to influential parents. These people can usually entice others to pitch in and help.

A *sample parent recruitment letter* appears on the following page. With some minor amendments and additions, you may be able to incorporate it into your volunteer recruitment plan.

SAMPLE LETTER

CHERRY HILL ELEMENTARY SCHOOL

April 5,19__

Dear Parents,

I am pleased to announce that on the evening of May 11, 19__ the children and staff of Cherry Hill Elementary School will present an exciting musical entitled *In Quest of Columbus*. All of us are looking forward to this event and hope we can call upon you for assistance. As you well know, a production of this scope requires a real team effort. With your support, we can continue to provide the students with a number of worthwhile enrichment activities.

In anticipation of your willingness to contribute some of your time to this endeavor, we have set aside three occasions when volunteers can lend assistance. On the evening of April 20, between the hours of 4:30 and 8:30 PM, a group of volunteers will meet in the gym to construct our background set. Those of you who have craft and woodworking skills would be most welcomed during this phase of the project. The painting of the set, along with the making of props, will take place in the all-purpose room on April 27 and 28 between the hours of 9:00 and 11:30 AM. Please feel free to join us at any time. It would be greatly appreciated if each volunteer could provide at least $1^{1/2}$ hours of assistance.

If it will be possible for you to assist us, please complete and return the response form that appears below to your child's homeroom teacher by April 15. In anticipation of your thoughtful consideration, I would like to extend to you our appreciation for your continued support and cooperation.

Sincerely,

Director of Theater Arts

— — — — — — — — — — — — — — DETACH AND RETURN BY APR. 15 — — — — — — — — — — — — — —
VOLUNTEER RESPONSE FORM

Please print   (Name of volunteer) _____   (Student's name) _____

Phone: (home)_____ (work)_____

Check the box adjacent to the date(s) you plan to lend assistance. Please include your approximate arrival time.

❑   April 20   arrival time _____

❑   April 27   arrival time _____

❑   April 28   arrival time _____

CHAPTER 9
GETTING THE JOB DONE

If you can appoint a volunteer to oversee the entire construction process, you will be free to concentrate on other aspects of your production.

Be sure to select a construction time that fits within a wide range of family schedules. Some groups find it best to work during the school day and others in the evening or on Saturday mornings.

Directors can maximize parental time and talent by dividing tasks into segments. Consult the previous example regarding the construction of the castle set. Try to ascertain the skill level of your volunteers and assign tasks accordingly. Be sure all essential tools and materials are on hand. Valuable time is lost when required items are not readily available.

Students

If the activity is safe, well organized, and carefully supervised, students can make significant contributions to set and prop construction. The key factor in working with students is to select a group of tasks well within their skill range. Young students should not be involved in any activities requiring tools not usually found in a typical classroom setting.

Over the years, I have enjoyed building a number of fairly sophisticated structures with children. In some instances the students have been as young as 9 years of age. On one occasion I involved a group of third graders in the construction of a geodesic dome which measured 8 feet high and 15 feet at the base. This was a large and a fairly

complex structure. The key to this successful project was having the children organized into small work groups. Each group was directed to work on one well-defined task. When a student tired of a specific task, he or she traded with a child who was assigned to another task group. By maintaining a chalkboard roster of tasks and students, we were able to successfully keep track of who was doing what. When the children changed work groups, they simply made the revision on the chalkboard roster.

When working with students, take some extra time to explain what is being made, how it will be made, and where it will be used. In order for them to share in your vision, students, like adults, need to know the purpose of the project in which they are engaged. If you faithfully observe the following considerations, you and your students will enjoy a successful and productive experience:

1. Assign students to tasks well within the range of their skills and abilities.

2. Never involve students in activities that place them at risk. A busy construction project is not a good environment in which to teach students about the use of new and possibly dangerous tools.

3. Vigilantly plan each step. Be sure to organize tasks into well-defined segments.

4. If the time frame for the completion of the project is tight, do not involve students. The probability of an

accident is greater when tasks must be completed in a hasty manner.

5. Do not involve more students than you can safely supervise.

Professional Staff Members

One particularly valuable source of volunteer assistance comes from within your organization. In this case, I am referring to staff members who choose, of their own volition, to participate in your production. Since these individuals are familiar with the students, as well as the practices and procedures of your organization, they are most welcomed.

In-house recruitment must be conducted on a person-to-person basis and should not be fortified with any form of pressure from supervisory personnel. When speaking to a prospective volunteer, take great care to mention the special gift he or she can contribute to your production. Refer to this talent as a special resource which is truly needed for the total success of the program.

Directors who work in school settings should be especially interested in recruiting the services of language arts, music, industrial arts, and fine arts teachers. With a bit of care and feeding, skilled professional staff members frequently can be encouraged to contribute their time and talents.

As with parent helpers, expectations and time frames should be conveyed clearly to your prospective volunteers. Successful directors are organized and present themselves as individuals who know what they are doing and where they are going. Everyone likes to be on a winning team. If you are generous in sharing the recognition you receive for your programs, you may be able to enlist a number of willing staff members who look forward to participating in your theatrical productions.

Custodial and Maintenance Personnel

There are two areas where custodial and maintenance personnel can be of great service to directors. They can be called upon to pick up the materials needed for set and prop construction and they can be asked to assist with the erection of the completed set. Frequently materials can be purchased at a discount if the order is placed by personnel who have access to organizational accounts maintained at local lumberyards and hardware stores.

As with professional staff members, try to keep your request on a person-to-person basis. While you should not rule out gaining supervisory assistance with enlisting the aid of non-instructional personnel, they are usually more cooperative if they feel that you have taken the time to ask for their help personally.

In some organizations, maintenance personnel are made available for set and prop construction. If you are new to your work environment, it may be worth your while to inquire.

Sometimes an unexpected early morning delivery of coffee and doughnuts goes a long way in gaining the cooperation of support personnel who should be given visible credit for any contributions they make to your production. If your organization publishes a monthly or quarterly report, do not forget to use this opportunity to commend your support personnel for any assistance they may have rendered.

Supervisors and Principals

Most supervisors and principals recognize the positive contribution that theatrical productions make to the quality of the total learning environment; however, there are still some whose support must be nurtured and cultivated. The full support of supervisory personnel can facilitate your efforts greatly. If your supervisor maintains an aloof, hands-off attitude toward your productions, it would be worth your while to take some steps to involve him or her in the process.

The first step in obtaining the support of your supervisor is to give credit openly for any contribution he or she makes. A small gesture such as approving a purchase request, visiting a rehearsal, or being present on the day of the performance should be emphasized and treated as a significant contribution. Once drawn into the process, most administrators are quick to recognize the political value of being associated with a successful undertaking.

If your supervisor has been supportive, do not take what he or she does for granted. It takes a great deal of effort to maintain a stable environment that is supportive of the arts. Do not fail to recognize and thank your supervisor publicly. The sincere assistance and cooperation of an immediate supervisor is a priceless commodity.

On a number of occasions, some directors have given principals or supervisors cameo roles in their productions. This is not only good public relations, it also helps to make him or her an active participant in the process. With a true vested interest in the success of the production, supervisors who are directly involved tend to make sure all available resources are placed at the disposal of the director. The children seem to enjoy it as well.

Service Organizations

Groups including parent organizations (P.T.O., P.T.A.), scouting groups, religious groups, and local service organizations can make a significant contribution to your production. Directors should attempt to identify the resources available from each organization. Service groups may have volunteers who are ready to pitch in, parent organizations may have funds they are willing to contribute, while other organizations may have access to inexpensive materials and equipment. An investigation of these possible resources is worth your time and attention.

Many groups openly seek worthwhile opportunities to offer services and resources to others. Since most of these groups plan their activities and budgets sometime in advance, it is necessary for you to make your requests known well before they will be needed. The suggested approach is to draft a letter describing your organization and delineating your schedule and needs. Theatrical productions addressing social issues such as substance abuse and homelessness are topical areas that draw a broad base of support from a number of sources. It is worthwhile to include any plans you may have to engage in productions which address themes of this nature.

LONG-TERM COMMITMENTS

If handled properly, you will soon find you do not have to begin at ground zero on every occasion when volunteer assistance is required. An available contingent of willing volunteers can be maintained if the director is sensitive to the reasons why individuals lend time and energy to a project. There are two major elements that contribute to the maintenance of a long-term volunteer commitment. The first element deals with the quality of your production. If your performances are successful and well-received, others will want to be a part of them. The second element relates to your willingness to share credit with others. This also involves a vigilant effort on your part to see that all contributors receive proper recognition.

Both verbal and written recognition should be given at each performance. In order not to detract from the program listing of the performers, a separate sheet containing the names and contribution of each volunteer should be distributed along with the program. The sheet should state that "this performance was made possible by the assistance of the many able and willing volunteers who contributed their time and talent to this endeavor."

At the conclusion of the performance, verbal recognition should be given to those who assisted with the production. While it is not advisable to announce individual names,

key organizations as well as supervisory personnel (formal members of the organization and volunteer coordinators) should be mentioned. Care must be taken to stress the critical role played by all of your volunteers.

Another aspect of long-term volunteer involvement is related to a sense of affiliation. If volunteers believe they are an integral component in the process, they will offer their services more readily. There are two basic ways directors can convey a true sense of affiliation. One way is to keep potential volunteers informed of up-coming productions. Providing them with the title and the anticipated time frames (production schedules) not only keeps them up-to-date, it will hopefully increase the number of individuals who will be available when you need them. The second way you can stimulate a sense of belonging is to embrace the same type of feeling that accompanies an old-fashioned barn-raising. Make each construction session a social event with cold drinks and coffee readily available to volunteers. Give them a sense of community and belonging by making sure you know all of their names and that they have been cordially introduced to each other.

Meaningful volunteer recruitment procedures require an ongoing commitment on the part of the director; in the end, however, these efforts yield long-term dividends that are distributed at a time when they are most needed.

NOTES